MW01493361

Cash Flow S.___ ___

Generate Monthly Income from Covered Calls & Dividends

by Randall Stewart

© Copyright 2018 Randall Stewart

All Rights Reserved

No part of this publication may be reproduced or transmitted
in any form or by any means, electronic, mechanical,
photocopying, recording, or otherwise, without the written prior
permission of the author.

Disclaimer

As stipulated by law, I cannot and do not make any guarantees about your ability to get results or earn any money from my ideas, information, tools or strategies.

I don't know you and, besides, your results in life are up to you. Agreed? I just want to help by giving you some great content, direction and strategies.

The risk of loss in trading securities and options can be substantial. Please consider all relevant risk factors, including your own personal financial situation, before investing or trading. Stocks and options do involve risk and are not suitable for all investors.

Use caution and always consult your accountant, lawyer or professional advisor before acting on this or any information related to a lifestyle change or your finances.

Past results of any individual trader or trading system published by the author are not indicative of future returns by that trader or system, and are not indicative of future returns which may be realized by you.

All strategies and examples are provided for informational and educational purposes only and should not be construed as investment advice under any circumstances. Such set-ups are not solicitations of any order to buy or sell a financial security. Any financial numbers referenced here should not be considered average earnings, exact earnings or promises for actual or future performance.

Table of Contents

Introduction

You may not understand the full value now, but by the time you complete this book you'll understand exactly how you could generate monthly cash flow from your stock investments and reach your financial goals that much faster.

All the insights, strategies and best practice tips in this book will blow your mind. Without hesitation, I can tell you that these are the most effective strategies to wealth creation in the stock market for the average investor. I can say this because over the past 10 years I have meticulously studied and interviewed many of the industry's educational experts and investment leaders. I know what truly works on a consistent basis and I also know what does not work and those pitfalls to avoid. I'll reveal all of those "secrets" to you in this book.

I'll be sharing some of the most revealing insights and tips from over two dozen nationally-recognized investment and financial educators. Their advice will provide you with a well-rounded perspective on how to best generate enough wealth to pay for a better lifestyle. I'll bet you dollars to donuts that you'll be enlightened by their take on how to best make money in various market conditions. Sound intriguing?

You'll hear more about my story, how I got started, what experts do and what YOU must do. You'll be introduced to the world of stock investing for cash flow and I'll provide you with the frameworks that help you think through and strategize your investing. You'll dive deep into the whole process of investing from finding great opportunities, assessing their potential, selecting an appropriate investment strategy and determining the right time for entering and exiting positions. This is what I call the FAST Approach to managing cash flowing investments.

This book will show you how to accelerate your wealth by using a combination of "Best of Breed" stocks, dividends and covered call option strategies. Don't worry, I'll take you by the hand and walk you confidently through each strategy.

As a side note, the finer details and in-depth examples of using covered call strategies is beyond the scope of this book. In my opinion, video is a better medium for picking up these key concepts and I'll provide you with a list of additional resources to check out according to your level of interest.

Although this book does not cover specific detailed examples of various option strategies you could use, you'll still be exposed to the key insights and best practice tips that'll give you a higher level of confidence to enter and exit the market. I'll walk you through a few case studies so that you have a better sense of how the strategies may play out. By the end of this book, you'll be able to prove to yourself that you are capable of doing it on your own without having to rely on others. Wouldn't that be great!

Fundamental to your success, is developing a championship mindset. That's why I take my time engaging you from the get-go in part one of your book to adopt the right mindset to learn and to win. From there, part two provides massive and invaluable content that'll change your life forever. Using a cash flow investment system, you'll learn everything you need to know to better position yourself in the markets and create a consistent stream of cash flowing into your piggy bank.

All of this material is intended to inspire, instruct and empower you on how to become a more successful stock investor using the same best practice approaches that many stock investment educators have embraced.

Take your time going through the material. Revisit concepts that upon first glance are foreign to you. Nothing great was built overnight. You'll find that your commitment, belief and efforts will bring you closer to generating the level of wealth that you aspire to create for you and your loved ones. This is just the beginning. And it's a great one.

I congratulate you for your commitment and desire in taking the steps necessary to change your life for the better and realize your dreams and goals. You've picked up a knowledge-based resource that can set you free financially.

But, why should you listen to me? I'm no internationally acclaimed investment "guru". I feel that it is important for you to understand where I'm coming from in writing this book.
First of all, I love to invest in stocks and I've been through the frustration of trying to figure out how to make consistent returns as the markets have trended higher and lower over the past 20 years. It used to drive me up the wall. Just like many of you I started out being self-taught. And like many of you, I've made and lost money as I was trying to figure out how to best invest my hard-earned dollars. Maybe you can relate?

Back in 2011, when the S&P 500 ended the year with no appreciable gains, I was fortunate enough to generate a double-digit portfolio return using the cash flow strategies and approaches outlined in this book. Isn't it high time that you jumped on the bandwagon. Would your family be impressed with those types of returns? Hot dog diggity, I know that mine was.

In fact, some of the strategies you'll pick up work better when the stock market is going nowhere. Frankly, almost any stock investor can make money when the markets are trending higher using a BUY and HOPE the price goes up strategy. However, it becomes more challenging using this approach when the market is stagnant. You've seen this, right?

I'm also an educator, having taught in the public-school system and the corporate world over the past several decades. Yes, I'm an old fart. I have an extensive background in online marketing in the health care arena, having developed several online courses for various sectors. I even went as far as obtaining my Mutual Fund and Insurance "Advisor" accreditation. Although I never did become a mutual fund pedlar, I did gain some greater insights into how the financial markets operate. Wouldn't you like to pick up some of those tidbits of financial market knowledge that'll make a positive difference in your future investments? You bet you would, right?

Sharing my wealth of knowledge comes second nature. But, more importantly helping individuals quickly grasp and retain fundamental concepts has been a primary focus in my educational career. I'm hardwired to share the wealth of knowledge that I've acquired over the years. This'll save you time in researching which investment approaches will give you the greatest chance of success while reducing risk. And protecting your hard-earned money is of paramount importance, wouldn't you agree?

As well, I'm no different than most of you. As mentioned, I'm not an investment guru, nor have I made millions of dollars investing in the stock market. Over the years I've struggled at times making ends meet and I've been frustrated trying to figure out what does and doesn't work in the stock market. Yes, I've made those costly mistakes that brought me close to financial ruin in the early days when I was knee high to a grasshopper. Fortunately, over the years I've reached out to various stock investment educators to gain a better understanding of what works on a consistent basis. Being mentored by some of the best educators in the market has accelerated my learning curve. Just a handful of tidbits of information from their bags of tricks has saved me both money and time down the road.

So, Who's This Book for?

There are three kinds of people in this world; those who can count and those who can't. So, let's take a look at who would benefit from the concepts being presented. People have different reasons for wanting to invest in the stock market. This resource is primarily intended for the novice stock investor. However, those who have some limited knowledge of stock investing and options trading would benefit from many of the concepts and strategies discussed in this book.

For some of you, it's not having to work your fingers to the bone for 40 hours per week to create your desired lifestyle. You may feel that the more you complain about your conditions of employment, the longer God makes you live. And you may also see the best part of going to work as being the commute back home at the end of the day. You would love to not have to depend on your employer for the money that you need. You're looking at being able to quit your job or jobs earlier and leave the salt mines. Some of you would realistically like to retire in 10-20 years or less AND be in control of your investments.

As you know, constipated people don't give a crap. And many employers fall into that category when it come to your financial well-being.

The second group of investors who would benefit from this resource are those who of you would like to generate enough cash flow to pay down consumer debt and decrease the stress of financial hardship on your family. Being able to give more to your family and spend more time with them and friends is of paramount importance.

Have you ever wondered why a slight tax increase costs you $200 and a "substantial" tax cut saves you 30 cents? It seems almost impossible to get ahead in today's financial world. Whoever said: "Nothing is impossible," never tried slamming a revolving door. There must be a better way.

And the third group of you would just like to follow the crowd. In other words, if everyone else is placing a portion of their savings in the stock market then so should you. Herd mentality and the fear of missing out on lucrative opportunities can become a strong motivational force that draws investors into the stock market.

In my case, it's a combination of all three. I've always been intrigued with the wealth-generation potential that the stock market can provide. And I've persevered over the years to put into place those systems that allow me to optimize my investments. The key word here is "optimize" as opposed to "maximize". Capital preservation and risk management go hand-in-hand with the concept of optimizing your returns. Greed and high-risk positions will eventually bite you in the gluteus maximus by trying to maximize your returns.

Whatever your reasons are, we're going to cover everything you need to know to become a successful cash flow investor. You can use this system for the rest of your life, well into your 70's. Just think of the impact on your income.

Who's It Not for?
Let me cut to the chase. Unfortunately, there are those of you who would not benefit from the knowledge and skills being shared in this book. Unfortunately, I won't be able to help:

- Those "know it all's" who are not coachable and are unwilling to improve their financial education. If you are not an active learner who would like to pick up some new wealth generation skills, then this book is not for you.
- Those "couch potatoes" who are not motivated to put in some effort in setting up the necessary trading accounts and systems. Initially, you'll need to set up your trading accounts online so that you control when you enter and exit the market. You'll also need to set up a few simple systems for reducing consumer debt, increasing your savings activity and identifying opportunities in the market.
- Those who have no interest in monitoring their positions on a regular basis so as to optimize their returns when opportunities occur. You should be willing to spend at least 10 minutes a day assuring that your investments are performing as anticipated.
- Those "get rich quick schemers" who believe that they can beat the markets and make a poop-load of money in a very short period of time. True. This program allows you to generate wealth faster over time by producing income from your cash flowing investments. However, at the forefront of this approach is that capital preservation and a conservative risk tolerance are of utmost importance.

I've always believed that anything worthwhile exploring requires some effort up front in order to set things in motion. Wouldn't you agree? This book will serve you well with the myriad of tips and insights designed to save you the frustration of trying to figure it out all on your own. I wish I had all of these insights that are included in this guide at my figure tips 20 years ago. It would have radically changed the way I invest, not to mention the speed at which I could generate wealth.

You may currently believe that you're so poor that you can't even afford to pay attention. I'm going to help you change that current reality. Change is good, but dollars are better. If you're ready to empower yourself with the skills and tools necessary to make more consistent returns whether the market is trending higher or lower, then read on.

How this Resource Is Organized:

You'll discover that natural flow of this book is divided into two sections. The first deals with helping you grow on a personal level from developing a championship mindset to getting your financial affairs in order prior to investing. The second section of the book introduces you to the FAST Approach to investing for cash flow. You'll pick up several dozen strategies and insights into how to identify opportunities, along with how to best time your entry and exit into positions.

How you approach going through the various chapters I'll leave up to you. You're the best judge as to how you best learn. If you feel that you're best served by following the logical flow of the book, then by all means go through it from cover to cover. If so, we'll touch on how to build your edge by initially creating a cash flow mindset, followed by picking up tips on how to better manage your financial affairs and finally you'll learn how to use the FAST Approach to create consistent cash flow. On the flip side, some of you may wish to start with a particular chapter of interest and prefer to bounce around the book's content according to your particular needs.

I encourage you to take your time going through the material. It will serve you well. And it will put you on the fast-track to success, whether that be knowing how to generate enough cash flow to retire on without having a million-dollar fortune or just being at peace with your financial affairs.

So, let me ask you, are you one of those investors who is ready for a change? Are you ready to discover how you can generate consistent cash flow into your investment accounts using some simple strategies? And are you ready for a hum dinger of an educational journey with some of the best financial educators out there? Let's get started by taking up the challenge. To your ongoing success as a cash flow investor.

Chapter 1 - The Challenge

Focus Questions:
1. What are the four wealth pillars?
2. What three investing myths dissuade most stock investors from taking action?
3. Upon which investment approach is the Accelerated Cash Flow System based?
4. What is the "velocity of your money" and how do you accelerate your wealth?

Stock Market Reality Check
The vast majority of stock market investors place their hard-earned dollars in the hands of a trusted mutual fund advisor, which is the traditional approach to investing in the markets. Many well-intentioned investors who followed the advice of their mutual fund advisors lost a substantial portion of their hard-earned capital during the stock market crashes of 2001 and 2008. You may have seen your portfolio decimated in the wake of these two major set-backs.

Many of these passive investors panicked, moving their money out of stocks and into cash or bonds, right when the markets started to rebound missing yet another opportunity to grow their investment portfolios. It does not take much to see that this collective ignorance has a long-term negative impact on one's ability to build wealth.

You may be asking yourself why bother trying to invest when I can't even get ahead. It will take me another 20 to 30 years to get back to even if a use a buy and hold - and pray approach to investing in the markets. I don't have this much time if I'm approaching retirement. And just as I think I've made some progress, I get hit by another market meltdown and my portfolio suffers yet another blow. How can I even fathom regaining control over my investments? Sound familiar?

I recall, a close colleague of mine during my public school teaching days foaming at the mouth as he expressed his frustration with his mutual fund advisor. His advisor had him switching from one fund to another over a 10-year period, chasing after returns. It was driving him up the wall. His overall portfolio grew only by the additional deposits he had made over the years. He was bitter about what was unfolding and felt at a loss over what he could do.

I too would be frustrated and disillusioned with a system that was supposed to build my wealth over time. What's even more aggravating are the lies that the financial services industry have been perpetrating over the decades about investing in the stock market.

Many mutual fund advisors and financial advisors tout that stocks in the S&P 500 Index have generated an average return of around 10% over the past 90 years. This lulls investors into thinking that the stock market produces consistently high returns with little or no volatility. However, they don't tell you that markets do not climb upwards in a straight line. The very nature of the stock market is that it is subject to wild swings, not until the waves of the ocean during a storm.

The fact is - average returns are not average and much less so today. Markets have changed due to a surge in equity and commodity volatility and uncertainty. Relying on old rules is a recipe for disaster.

According to **James O'Shaughnessy** in his classic guide to the best-performing investment strategies of all time **What Works on**

Wall Street: "Seventy percent of the mutual funds covered by Morningstar fail to beat the S&P 500 over almost any 10-year period because their managers lack the discipline to stick with one strategy. This lack of discipline devastates long-term performance."

So, why is it that some actively-engaged investors are able to generate double digit returns on their money in the stock market in a year like 2011, yet most mutual fund investors lost money over the same period?

In 2011 the S&P 500 Index started and ended the year flat with no appreciable gains and most mutual fund investors ended up with a loss at year's end. However, a little stock investment knowledge allows the informed active investor great wealth creation opportunities despite what the markets were doing.

Watching your investment portfolio being decimated by the markets and not knowing how you can capitalize on great investment opportunities as they unfold is both disheartening and discouraging. You may feel completely at a loss and totally helpless in not being able to do a thing about your investments when the normal market volatility takes its toll on your holdings. Panic may set in. And in the heat of panic you may move out of positions only to realize that you've once again missed a great opportunity.

This deception about how the markets really function is often not taken into consideration in one's overall investment plan, especially in the short term. Without truly knowing how the markets function you are unable to incorporate money-making strategies that capitalize on the normal fluctuations of the stock market. This is what you'll learn how to do by the end of this book - on my boy scout's honor.

Being Kicked to the Curb:

After having spent several decades in the teaching profession, in both the public-school system and private enterprise, my wife Cindy and I were in the fortunate position to retire much earlier than anticipated. We were finally in the enviable position of being time rich and had started to create those lasting memories with our travels, pursuing our passions for the wine and food culture, and being able to recreate in the great outdoors of the Pacific Northwest.

Then our dream lifestyle and financial world came crashing down all around us. Not because of having invested in the stock market, nor real estate. We had invested the majority of our capital with a financial investment organization that was heavily invested in the precious metals industry, consumer debt collection and green earth energy technologies.

The international investment portfolio that I was managing showed significant double digit returns in the early years. All was well. We could afford to retire early and enjoy a time-rich lifestyle that few people attain now-a-days. Unbeknownst to us, our hard-earned money had disappeared soon after it left our hands. We were the victims of an elaborate investment scam that not only affected our lives, but the lives of thousands of innocent investors across North America. Talk about being kicked in the "yichees". Ouch! To add insult to injury, during the 2-year period of time that the scam was slowly unraveling and our cash flow from the investments dried up, we ate through the balance of our capital ear-marked for other investment opportunities.

The realization that our dreams had been shattered was devastating. Yes, I was madder than a box of frogs. We now had the arduous task of trying to figure out a way to build back the equity that we had lost. How could we re-build the hundreds of thousands of dollars necessary to retire comfortably? And how could we possibly do it within a 10 to 15-year period of time while we were still capable of working? At the time, I had all the money I would ever need, - that is if I died by four o'clock that afternoon. Maybe you can relate?

Cindy and I had some tough choices to make. The first order of business was to immediately temporarily down-size our lifestyle, get back into the workforce and start amassing more investment funds. We scraped and saved every penny that we could in order to get back on our feet. I wasn't going to let this financial blow dictate the direction of my future, living off of government assistance and working well into my 70's in order to just survive. As much as I love Wal-Mart as a business model, I wasn't planning on spending my retirement years as a front-door greeter.

I knew that prior to investing my money with these scam artists, I had had some great success in picking winning stocks and building a significant stock investment portfolio over time. It was also one reason why I was able to initially retire early.

But how could I get back to where I was in less than 15 years?

I spent the next two years learning how to invest in stocks, real estate and precious metals. I became a consummate researcher, now having read over 150 books and taken over a dozen different investment courses. During 2010 and 2011, I learned how to accelerate my money-making in the stock market under all market conditions, whether the market was heading up, going no-where or undergoing a correction. It was at that time that I had my Aha moment. I came to realize that cash flow and not amassing a huge nest egg was the key to fulfilling my dreams and maybe yours as well. That made me happier than a clam at high tide.

If you would like to achieve similar results then nod your head YES! I know I can't see you, but I want you to make sure that you're participating - it's important don't you think! So, nod your head YES!

Before we delve into how to achieve a consistent stream of cash flowing into your investment accounts, let's take a look at the three types of investments that all wealth builders have.

What Do Wealth Builders Do?

The majority of self-made millionaires focus their time and energy on three types of smart investments, namely:

1. Their ongoing financial education in specific areas that will have a direct impact on their ability to grow their capital under all market conditions.
2. Their ability to acquire cash flowing assets, whether it be in the stock market, real estate or certain commodities.
3. Their ability to build systematized businesses that are able to generate passive income while they sleep.

Let's take a quick look at each of these smart investment vehicles and how they might help you down the road.

Vehicle #1: Become Financially Intelligent.

By picking up a copy of this book, you have taken the first step to building your wealth. Your curiosity has paid off. It has been a motivational factor in moving you closer to realizing your dreams. The fact that you have taken the time to explore ways of improving your current financial situation says a lot about who you are.

It's more and more challenging to pursue the American Dream. Why? Because you have to be asleep to believe it. However, you have stepped from the realm of the "wanna be" wealth dreamer who is all talk and no action - to having made a conscious decision to actually do something about your financial affairs. Now it's time to start creating wealth for you and your loved ones. And, it all begins with the most important tool that you can develop - your financial intelligence.

Increasing your financial intelligence over time will empower you to solve the money problems that you may be faced with at this moment. By improving the quality of the financial information that you use in your decision-making and differentiating between fact and opinion you set yourself up to be in a better position to tap into your financial genius. And in the following chapter we'll explore how you can tap into your full potential as an investor.

Vehicle #2: Acquire Assets.
The second smart investment vehicle is to acquire assets that put money into your pockets. In other words, invest in those asset classes with a proven track record of generating cash flow from the investment.

The top three general asset classes that most people are familiar with as investment opportunities are equities, real estate and commodities. This book delves into the world of stock investing and shows you step-by-step how to implement an accelerated cash flow investment system that systematically puts money into your pocket.

The second general asset class that active investors like to invest in is real estate. A common cash flow approach in real estate is to buy an investment property and then rent it out as a means of generating a monthly income. Coincidentally, this is similar to the covered call strategy of "renting out" your stock in the options market, whereby you receive a monthly cash premium for doing so.

And finally, the third asset class is that of investing in commodities such as oil wells, precious metals mines or alternative energy ventures that can provide a monthly check.

Each of these asset classes has specific benefits, risks and rewards.

For most investors who are trying to build or re-build their wealth the most cost-effective and time-efficient way to generate cash flow is through the stock market. As your wealth begins to accumulate, you may wish to further explore investing in rental real estate or specific commodity plays since these investment classes tend to be a little more capital intensive to start off with.

Whether you choose equities, real estate or commodities as your preferred asset class, please keep in mind that your focus should be on putting money into your pocket through positive cash flow. If most of the stock analysts look favorably upon those businesses that have the ability to generate ongoing cash flow, why wouldn't you want to emulate what they value most - an increasing stream of incoming cash?

Vehicle #3: Build Systematized Businesses.

I mention the third smart investment vehicle, only to give you a complete perspective of the three major areas where the resources of effective wealth builders can be allocated for creating sustainable wealth.

For the highly motivated individual, the option of building a low-start-up cost, systemized business that runs on its own even when you're not present is appealing. It's definitely one effective way to exit the rat race from a 9 to 5 job, be the master of your own destiny and not succumb to your employer's chosen path for you.

A word of caution though - be aware that starting any business requires hard work and patience. Don't confuse "get rich quick", which is a distinct possibly for you, with "get rich easy". Unfortunately, there are too many self-promoting experts who'll tell you differently, especially those that are flaunting a particular product or service. Over the years I have come across several online marketers who have been touting the same message:" Blogging is easy. I'll show you how to get a blog up and running in less than one hour and then you'll see the money rolling in." Don't let anyone try to fool you into thinking that building any business is easy.

Of course, on the flip side of this coin is the wealth creation potential that you can tap into should you have realistic expectations and develop an appropriate business attitude that factors in the amount of time and effort required to build your second or third stream of income. Makes sense, right?

Insights to Consider:
Having an understanding of these three smart investing options in the back of your mind, you'll begin to assess opportunities and make money allocation decisions in a different light.

For example, my wife Cindy and I have come to an understanding that our hard-earned dollars are channeled into investments that either improve our level of financial education or purchase an appreciating cash flowing asset. When we have appropriately allocated our monetary resources towards building our dreams, it provides us with a greater sense of accomplishment, confidence, ongoing motivation and hope for a better future for the two of us.

You too can walk a similar path to financial freedom.

Now that you have an idea as to where you can channel your future efforts, let's take a look at what you need in order to succeed as a cash flow investor.

The Four Wealth Pillars:
I also came to understand that in order to build sustainable wealth over time; I needed to channel my efforts into four specific areas, which I call my wealth pillars.

Pillar #1: Increasing my savings for investment purposes.
Everything hinges on the first pillar. If you do not make saving for investing a priority - you cannot invest - if you cannot invest - you cannot create the lifestyle that you dream about. During the course of this book, we'll explore several simple approaches that'll get you headed in the right direction. The first pillar to wealth creation remains your ability to move capital into investment opportunities as a result of your saving to invest regime.

Pillar #2: Investing in individual top-quality, dividend-paying stocks.
This strategy over time will prove to be the simplest way to generate massive wealth when coupled with renting out your stock in order to generate ongoing cash flow. Yes, you heard me right, renting out your stock to other investors willing to pay you for the privilege.

For example, back in 2010, I invested in Qualcomm, which supplies many of the mobile internet companies with their components. Within a 6-month period of time I managed to capture two dividend payments, monthly covered call premiums and a 30% appreciation in the price of the stock before moving on to the next best investment opportunity.

The reason why I am sharing this example with you is not to boast about my particular investment prowess. It's to give you an idea as to the potential of learning how to accelerate your wealth through stock investing.

Pillar #3: Investing in "Best of Breed" stocks.

As you will see, this pillar will become a structural part of your wealth creation machine. Buying stock of those businesses that are the market leaders in their sector lends itself to a higher probability that the shares will appreciate in value more so than average stocks in that sector. The market likes businesses that have solid growth in earnings and cash flow.

For example, should you find a fundamentally solid stock that doesn't offer a dividend, you can employ a few simple covered call option strategies that will generate a monthly cash flow into your brokerage account.

Pillar #4: Selling option contracts on stock that you own.

This pillar piggy backs off of the previous two. It's the sale of options contracts on stock that you already own. In essence, you receive a cash premium in your brokerage account when you agree to sell your stock shares at a specific price on or before a pre-determined date.

I'll show you how you can generate a monthly flow of cash into your account, by renting out your stock similar to how a property owner rents out an apartment unit. The process of selling covered calls can generate a conservative monthly cash flow of 2 to 3 percent when properly structured, which is what you'll learn how to do by the end of this book.

You too can do it!

The average knowledgeable investor can follow in my footsteps, or those of the experts who are showcased in this resource, and do exactly what I have been so fortunate to realize. By learning how to use simple investment strategies coupled with time-tested approaches, you'll be able to head down the path to financial freedom that'll eventually lead to fulfilling your dreams.

You may be asking yourself: So, if these strategies can consistently produce double digit returns over the long haul why don't more people follow a similar system? Why aren't more people getting rich from investing in the stock market?

Which brings us to the most destructive myths in the financial service industry that dissuade people from taking action and becoming cash flow generating machines in the stock market.

The 3 Biggest Myths:

Myth #1: You need over $1 million to retire comfortably.

Unfortunately, we've all been brain-washed into thinking that we need to amass a huge nest egg in order to live comfortably during our retirement years. This is based on the assumption that we move our investment capital into more conservative investment vehicles such as bonds, treasury notes or certificates of deposit as we approach retirement.

With these so-called "safer, risk-free" investments, we can count on a whopping 2-4% annual return that just beats inflation. It's no wonder that many financial advisors want you to have over $1 million in tangible assets. If you're only getting a conservative return of 3%, this equates to a retirement income of $30,000 per year.

There must be a better way. So how do you take back control over your wealth creation?

The simple answer - learn how to invest for cash flow, whether it be in the stock market, real estate, systematized businesses or even commodities. You may be asking yourself: "Now that would require a whole shift in how I've been programmed to think and act." I know that it took me awhile to fully grasp the possibility of a simpler approach to dealing with my lack of retirement capital challenge.

For example (and a simplified one at that), in order to realize an income of $30,000 per year with a 15% return on your capital, you would only need to position $200,000, not a $1 million in the stock and options markets. That's a huge difference! And do-able for most Americans to realize. It's a far cry from what many in the financial services industry have been saying that you need. Sure, I've given you a simplistic version of what could transpire. But it does illustrate how you could realistically create a cash flowing system with a smaller capital base.

By becoming an active investor, you can continue to build your wealth well into your 70's. As long as you can think clearly, you can profit from being actively involved in generating cash flow from your investments.

This entails building your investments around individual stocks and using simple options strategies to both protect your positions and generate additional cash flow. Much of this book will focus on how you can empower yourself to generate consistent double digit returns through efficient and effective cash flow strategies. Once you have your cash machine in place, you can either systematically tap into the income being generated or allow it to compound over time.

Myth #2: Options trading is too complicated and too risky for the average investor.

True, getting started in options can be daunting. What scares many investors off is the specialized language unique to options trading. As in learning any new skill, the learning curve can be steep.

However, once you have acquired those basic skills, being able to apply that newfound wisdom to increase your ability to make money whether the stock market is going up, down or sideways is well worth the effort. Once you master the special language and start using a few conservative money-making option strategies, you'll wonder why more investors don't do the same thing.

Jay Pestrichelli and **Wayne Ferbert** in their book **Buy and Hedge** which marries stock investing with options trading say that: "Hedging your investments changes how you measure risk in your portfolio. It simplifies the process. When you are hedged, you have controlled for your risk."

Hedging is a term often used to describe the use of either a call or put option to reduce the risk of capital loss, in other words to provide some insurance for your stock holdings. Renting out your stock to other investors - in other words - selling covered calls provides you with both an opportunity to generate additional cash flow as well as cushion your stock from the effects of a temporary drop in the stock price. In effect, options can be used to reduce your overall portfolio risk and make you some additional cash at the same time.

Scott Kyle in his book **The Power Curve**, in which he advocates smart investing by using dividends, options and the magic of compounding states that: "Depending on stock and volatility levels, you can often generate 1.5X to 3X in options premium over what is paid in the form of a dividend. For example, if you buy Company X that pays a 5% dividend, you can reasonably generate another 7% to 15% of incremental income annually through the sale of options. During high VIX environments (VIX is a measure of volatility in the markets) the amount of income available from options sales can easily exceed 20% annually."

Who wouldn't want to learn how to generate returns of 20% just from their options plays?

Myth #3: The higher the returns the riskier the investment.

Before looking at how specific investment vehicles fair in terms of risk assessment, let's take a look at what are the different types of risk that we need to factor into our assessment process.

Market risk:
Market risk refers to the upward and downward price movement in the short-term of the asset being traded, whether it is in stocks, bonds, real estate, commodities or currencies. This concept is known as price volatility and each market has a historical range of price fluctuations that define its level or degree of risk.

Interest Rate Risk:
This risk is a result in a change in the value of the investment with rising or falling interest rates.

Inflation Risk:
Inflation risk or purchasing power risk is due to an expansion of the money supply that causes goods and services to rise in price.

Lack of Control Risk:
When you relinquish control over your investment, you also increase your risk of being able to adapt quickly to changing

circumstances, such as a market meltdown. Not being able to influence investment decisions that'll have a huge impact on your holdings poses a major risk to your ongoing investment success.

Lack of Liquidity Risk:
When your capital is tied up in an investment that locks your money in for a fixed period of time, you can't take advantage of better investment opportunities down the road. These lost opportunity costs are a risk factor that you need to consider before locking in any capital for a period of time. This is especially crucial when the investment does not allow you to have access to your principal until the end of the holding period.

Strategy Risk:
Strategy risk occurs when you mismatch your investment objective with the type of strategy that you are using to achieve this objective. This commonly occurs when you change your intended time frame for holding your investment. Many impatient investors succumb to this type of risk - selling when they should be holding longer or buying on hype in the news without checking out the stock.

Lack of Proper Diversification Risk or Correlation Risk:
Correlation in the stock market refers to the degree to which two stock holdings have a tendency to change together. If you are holding stocks that move up or down in unison under a variety of market conditions, this increases your exposure to market risk. To reduce the effects of correlation risk, the smart investor diversifies his overall investment portfolio across asset classes, such as stocks, real estate and commodities, which normally do not have a high trading correlation to each other. Should one market go down, in all likelihood, the market for another asset class is heading up. We'll look at a few ways of reducing this type of risk later in the book.

Six Investment Approaches:

Having briefly touched on seven common types of risk associated with investing, let's take a look at how they size up against six different investment approaches, starting with the most common fixed-income investment - the bond.

Approach #1: Bonds.

Many advisors in the financial services industry advocate placing your money in fixed-income investments such as bonds, especially as you approach retirement.

A typical bond allocation strategy is to set aside a percentage of your overall portfolio for bonds using an age factor. A common calculation is to subtract your age from 110 or 100 to arrive at the percentage of your portfolio that should be in stocks, with the balance in bonds. For example, if you are 50 years old, the formula recommends having between 50-60% of your money in stocks. Therefore, you should have 40-50% of your capital in bonds.

Bonds have traditionally been thought of as being a safe haven compared to stocks, which appear to fluctuate more dramatically in price. But, are bonds really "safer" than stocks?

That depends on what you mean by safer. Successful investing, where you are able to generate consistent inflation-beating returns over the long term, depends on a number of important factors.

One key factor is the effects of inflation. Any investment that is unable to at least keep up with the pace of inflation is risky. You jeopardize the purchase power of your initial capital in the future by not seeking investment vehicles that at least keep up with the rate of inflation as is the case with a savings account that pays much less than the current rate of inflation. Inflation typically rises as long-term interest rates climb.

Bond yields and bond prices have an inverse relationship to each other. When interest rates rise; the price and value of your long-term bonds falls. As well, your bonds get paid back with cheaper dollars due to the effects of inflation thus eroding your purchasing power.

In today's economic climate, long-term bonds with their current low yields of 3 to 4% barely keep up with the rate of inflation. At a 3 percent interest rate, it will take you over 23 years to double your initial investment. That's a lot longer than what most investors are willing to wait nowadays.

Over the long term you will experience an erosion of your purchasing power by being too heavily weighted in any fixed-income investments. Does this sound like a risk-free investment choice to you?

Approach #2: Mutual Funds.
We all want to be able to build our little nest egg over time without a loss of our purchasing power. The stock market has provided the safest opportunity to do so over time, which brings us to the next most common and popular investment vehicle, the mutual fund.

The mutual fund industry has been booming for decades. Billions have been made for both the fund managers and salesmen despite the industry's lack luster performance in comparison to the S&P 500 or DJIA. More than 70 percent of mutual fund managers are unable to consistently beat the broad market indexes such as the S&P 500 over time. Thus, average returns for mutual funds, once you account for fees, have historically been around 5 to 6%, once again just above the rate of inflation.

Unfortunately, many financial advisors will only sell you investments that generate a commission for themselves, and not necessarily the best opportunities for higher returns for you. You'll end up making your advisor rich well before you do. From my point of view that makes as much sense as putting a screen door on a submarine.

The returns of most actively-managed mutual funds fail to keep up with the market averages. When you factor in a Management Expense Ratio (MERs) of 1.5 - 3.5 % of assets per year that all actively-managed mutual funds charge, you significantly reduce your returns over the long term. Also, as the value of the investment rises, the MER represents an increasing dollar amount that is paid out.

Sales charges or "loads" as high as 5% that are paid to the advisor either up front or on the back end further reduce your returns. These numbers are not reflected in the posted returns of mutual funds. With a back-end load fund, in the event that you close your account prior to a specified holding period, which is usually 5 or 6 years long, you're charged back additional percentages for not keeping your money in that fund. This is just another level of risk that you need to account for as a mutual fund investor.

As well, when you buy mutual funds you're placing the control of your investment decisions in the hands of a fund manager who in all likelihood will underperform the broad market and whose investment approach may fly directly in the face of your desired objectives.

Approach #3: Index Funds.

A better alternative to mutual funds may be the Index Mutual Fund or Exchange Traded Index Fund (ETF) that holds a basket of stocks representing an index such as the S&P 500 or Russell 1000. The index fund attempts to spread the volatility of individual stocks across a huge portion of the market by creating a portfolio of the largest companies in the market. The idea is that by diversifying your holdings across the entire market you reduce your overall risk of having say one stock severely underperforming the others in a small portfolio of 10 holdings.

Since these funds are not actively managed the fees associated with owning them are much less than actively managed mutual funds. Hence, they are able to generate returns that are just below the market averages. These funds have historically generated returns in the range of 7 to 8%.

At this rate of return you could expect to double your portfolio in about 10 years if all goes well and the markets do not experience a couple of major corrections in the same decade as in 2001 and 2008 or the recent minor correction in 2018.

Approach #4: Individual Stocks.

Historically, owning a well-diversified portfolio of individual stocks has generated average returns of 9 to 10%, which is consistent with what you would expect the broad market to experience. This is the arena where the majority of actively-engaged stock investors begin their journey into the wonderful world of stock investing. In the hands of a knowledgeable and experienced investor these returns can creep up into the realm of double digit returns.

However, without the use of options positions, the stock investor must be very adept in moving into positions when the stocks are undervalued and out of positions when the stocks are overpriced.

The biggest challenge is dealing with strategy risk. One common mistake is where an investor enters a short-term trade position that heads in the wrong direction and rather than cut one's losses the investor simply switches his strategy, which now becomes a long-term buy and hope it rebounds position.

The individual stock investor must diligently account for correlation risk in his or her portfolio, as well as market risk, which shows up in the wild swings that characterize how the stock market functions.

Given a historic return of 10%, an actively-engaged investor can expect to double his or her money in about 7 years. Not bad, but can we do better?

Approach #5: Accelerated Cash Flow Approach.
Moving up the food chain of investment options, we arrive at the accelerated cash flow approach to investing, which combines the power of individual stock picks with options positions. A knowledgeable cash flow investor can comfortably generate double digit returns, over long periods of time, in the range of 15 to 20% depending on the strategies employed.

Unfortunately, I can't make you any promises as to what sort of returns you'll generate. Promises are like babies. They're fun to make, but harder to deliver.

The major advantages of combining individual stock picks with options is that you're able to take advantage of the compounding effects of dividends, option premiums, and stock appreciation, as well as being able to mitigate your downside risk through the use of strategically placed positions.

The challenge of course is in increasing your financial education to a level where you can profit from a combination of simple yet effective strategies to generate massive cash flow.

As with buying individual stocks, the cash flow investor must mitigate correlation risk.

The massive appeal of the accelerated cash flow approach to investing is that you're able to rapidly increase your rate of being able to double your holdings, typically within a 4 to 5-year period.

Approach #6: Options Trading.
And last but not least is the world of options trading, which is a double-edged sword. Trading options as a day trader can be very lucrative and rewarding with annual returns upwards of 24%.

However, it has ruined more lives than created wealth because individuals have not taken the time to learn how to effectively trade options and more importantly how to change their mindset to become disciplined, focused and confident traders.

As **Mark Douglas** in his book **Trading in the Zone** so succinctly puts it: "The goal of any trader is to turn consistent profits on a regular basis, yet so few people ever really make consistent money as traders. What accounts for the small percentage of traders who are consistently successful? To me, the determining factor is psychological - consistent winners think differently from everyone else."

Why the Accelerated Cash Flow Investment System?

An accelerated cash flow investment system focuses on creating your winning edge. That edge is simply a higher probability of one outcome occurring over others. You'll learn step-by-step how to build a winner's mindset in the coming chapters.

As you can see, risk comes in many different flavors. You risk losing purchasing power if your investment vehicle is unable to keep up with the rate of inflation, as is the case with most fixed-income investments. You risk being able to generate higher returns because of fees that eat away at your potential capital growth as is the case with mutual funds. You also lose control over how you want to invest and in what investments by turning over the reins to a fund manager. You risk having to wait decades in order to build up any appreciable wealth through index funds. And, you must also resign yourself to amassing a fortune before being able to retire since you have not learned how to generate consistent double-digit returns under various market conditions.

The only risk that faces you now is in committing the time and undertaking the challenge of becoming a cash flow Investor. By taking up this challenge, your odds of becoming wealthy over time increase dramatically. This cash flow investment system is based on two key factors that will accelerate your wealth building process even faster.

Focus on Two Key Wealth Building Factors:

Joe Terranova in his book "***Buy High Sell Higher***" says: "Most investors buy a stock with little thought as to how long they will hold onto it. In addition, few give more than a passing thought to what kind of return they are looking for from any given investment. As a result, they intentionally or unintentionally subscribe to the buy and hold theory of investing, hanging onto assets come hell or high water. Few of us can afford to be like

Warren Buffett and hold a stock forever while it dips into negative territory and drags down the rest of our portfolio. Before you invest in any asset, you first need to ask yourself: How long you are willing to tie up your capital with it?"

The critical question that you need to be asking yourself is when do you need to move to another investment opportunity with more strength and momentum that allows you to accelerate your wealth-building? Which brings us to the first key wealth-building factor.

Factor #1: Increasing the Velocity of Your Money.

Truly successful investors do not park their money and forget about it. They move their money around into better and better opportunities. This is true whether you are talking about stocks, real estate or other business opportunities. This strategy is known as the "velocity of your money."

Your goal in investing should be to acquire cash flowing assets and to continually seek better opportunities that will get you closer to realizing your dreams. The old buy and hold strategy that worked during the last major bull market of 2012 to 2017 no longer works.

As **Joe Terranova** in his book "**Buy High Sell Higher**" states: "If the buy and hold strategy continued to work one would be able to buy the S&P 500 Index in 2000 and ride the escalator up to higher profits by 2010. That was not the case. The S&P 500 was down roughly 10% in the last decade."

If such is the case, we need to consider those strategies that'll work in today's markets that have experienced surges in equity and commodity volatility, not to mention the increased uncertainty.

In order to accelerate your wealth building process, you have two plans of attack to consider:

The first is to look at how you can increase the velocity of your money within investments. This entails maximizing your profit-making potential by focusing on the combination of dividend payments, option premiums and stock appreciation in your core holdings. Each component adds to your overall return compounding over time to quickly reach a point of critical mass.

The second plan of attack to increase the velocity of your money is between investments. When you get into the habit of monitoring possible opportunities, the odd one could present itself when it meets your specific buy criteria. It is at this point in time that you need to act quickly to move your money in order to take advantage of that window of opportunity.

By creating a winning mindset and planning your investments in advance you increase the chances of moving into these profitable opportunities.

Factor #2: Reaching Critical Mass.

I briefly mentioned the concept of reaching a point of critical mass with your investments. Let me elaborate. When you start out investing, the compounding effect of your investing slowly builds over time. At a certain point, the compounding effect of your cash flow that you're generating from your investments will exceed your annual household expenses and provide you with your desired lifestyle. It is at this point in time that you have reached a point of critical mass with your investing. This number is different for each and every one of us.

Once you have reached this point of investing prowess, you can now look forward to reaching your financial freedom day that much sooner. That is my objective - to share with you the wealth of knowledge of the top investment educators currently engaged in the market today through an accelerated cash flow investment system.

Seven Things Great Investors Do:

Being on top of your game all the time as a stock market investor has its challenges. What does it take to consistently earn money in the markets today? Here are 7 golden nuggets of wisdom to help get you closer to your investment goals:

Tip #1: Have a positive, "will try hard" attitude all the time. Commit to learning something new about stock investing every day. Be proactive and develop some positive daily learning habits. Set aside some time each morning to stimulate and challenge your mental capacity by reading for fifteen to twenty minutes or listening to an audio book before heading off to work or elsewhere. This tip alone will empower you to be a more consistent and successful investor.

Tip #2: Show a willingness to learn. Be teachable and keep an open mind to learning about the incredible world of investing. You can teach an old dog new tricks. Learning forces you to step out of your "comfort zone" and change the way you think about yourself, others and the wonderful world of investing.

Tip #3: Ask, listen and learn. Use the acronym A.S.K. – Always Seeking Knowledge – to guide you. Let your curiosity take hold of you and move you to another level of understanding about investing by tapping into the wealth of knowledge of those experts who have gone before you. Actively go out and seek answers to your most pressing questions either on blogs, video posts or forums.

Tip #4: Be creative in how you squeeze learning time into your daily routine. Can you combine your exercise time with reading or listening to a personal development tape? How about listening to an audio program while walking the dog or on your morning commute?

Tip #5: Be organized and tidy with your investment information. Keeping your desk area and any investment resource material tidy fosters both increased productivity and greater motivation to stay engaged in learning how to become a better investor. No longer will you get frustrated not knowing where key documents are kept and give up on the whole investment process.

Tip #6: Avoid the time waster of blaming yourself, others or you dog for mistakes you make with your investments. Mistakes ultimately result in an opportunity to learn. Focus on the lessons learned from your failures. Every potential investment presents itself as a unique self-contained opportunity at that particular moment. Keep this in mind for all of your future investment opportunities.

Tip #7: In general, become more of a problem solver. Think of ways to apply what you've just learned. Continuously engage your mind in solving problems or overcoming obstacles in order to achieve greater success. Ask yourself: How could I use this newfound knowledge right now? At the end of each day, reflect on what you've learned and all those little successes you've experienced.

By following these golden nuggets of wisdom, you set yourself up to become a truly great investor.

Start Creating a Championship Mindset:

Creating a championship mindset starts with your core belief about your abilities. A key component to success is being able to grow towards reaching your maximum potential.

Do YOU believe in your potential?

To work towards reaching your full potential, keep these points in mind:

1. Reaching your potential requires focus on your goals, which means that you'll need to concentrate on those elements that benefit your growth and sacrifice those factors that take you away from achieving your full potential. Give your energy and your time only to those elements that draw you closer to your life purpose.
2. Concentrate your efforts on continuously learning and growing for the better. To improve the quality of your life and those around you, improve yourself.
3. Forget what has transpired in the past and focus on what you need to do for reaching your full potential. We cannot change the past. Rather, look for the lessons that may be learned from your past experiences.
4. Talk is cheap. Start working towards developing your full potential today. Commit to your self-development, which will bring you closer to realizing your life purpose.
5. Keep challenging and pushing your preconceived boundaries or "comfort zone." True growth occurs only when you step out of your set and familiar ways and dare yourself to achieve and improve. Model growth and a willingness to change and move out of your comfort zone.
6. Enjoy and celebrate your accomplishments and successes. Reward yourself from time to time, such as going out to dinner in a fancy restaurant or spending an hour at a spa.

7. Create a positive growth environment for you and those with whom you work or live. Surround yourself with people from whom you can learn. Develop an affirming, supportive and caring demeanor.

My primary goal is to provide you with the essential concepts required for you to begin your success journey, coupled with some of the most effective learning strategies to bring about meaningful, long-term change.

The first step in your journey is to get in touch with your true self and unleash the incredible potential that is within you now. Always remember you're unique, just like everyone else. Let's get started with exploring how shifting your beliefs and attitudes about money and investing will dramatically increase your ability to consistently make money in the markets. Your next chapter, Developing Your Cash Flow Mindset, awaits you now.

Chapter 2 - Developing Your Cash Flow Mindset

Focus Questions:
1. What investment goals do I have?
2. What is my relationship with money and wealth?
3. How is fear holding me back from being a successful investor?
4. What could I be doing to better focus on wealth creation?
5. What rules should I follow, if any, when entering and exiting positions in the market?

This chapter will give you a new paradigm for what it takes to become a great investor. A paradigm is a way of seeing something. It is a viewpoint from which you can operate that empowers you to make quantum leaps in the areas of growth and achievement. My goal is to help you reach your full potential as an investor and ultimately build your confidence in your investing ability. Yes, you can do it on your own without turning your savings over to a "Mutual Fund Salesman".

What Investment Goals Do You Have?
We all set goals on a daily basis in order to accomplish our day-to-day tasks and move closer to completing projects that we may have on the go. According to *Dr. Heidi Grant Halverson* in her groundbreaking book *Succeed: How We Can Reach Our Goals* your goals can be grouped into two question categories - "why" goals and "what" goals.

Why goals align well with our core desires; those things that we truly desire and resonate with us at a deeper level. Why goals tend to focus on achieving a specific state of being down the road, whether that be a desired lifestyle or accomplishment. You may have caught yourself asking "Why am I doing this?" as a subtle reminder of a longer-term objective that you've set for yourself that has some distinct benefits to you down the road. Dreaming about the big picture has its benefits in helping you move in the right direction; however, "why" goals provide little support when dealing with new or difficult-to-learn tasks.

Which brings us to the importance of "what' goals. What goals tend to focus on those steps or tasks that you need to follow immediately in order to arrive at a specific outcome. When you focus on what needs to be done first, followed by the second step and then subsequent steps, you're more likely to tackle challenging tasks. Learning how to invest requires that you focus most of your attention on "what" goals as you learn new knowledge and skills. Dr. Halverson points out that by focusing on the "what" in skill development, you're more likely to stick with a program and realize your goals over time.

Working through this book will require both a time commitment to the process and a willingness to learn new skills and approaches. Start by setting some specific step-by-step "what" goals that'll move you closer towards your "why" goals and your core desire. To begin with, you may wish to outline those days and times in your appointment calendar or daily planner that you'll set aside for this book. Then take a look at how you can realistically structure your week to apply the research skills and various strategies that you've just been exposed to in each chapter.

I encourage you to challenge yourself by setting realistic expectations, yet demanding goals. Research has shown that if you believe that your goal is easily attainable, you're less likely to succeed because you'll apply less effort, be less focused and have a lower level of on-going commitment. By challenging yourself, you've not only a higher chance of success in achieving those demanding goals, but also the psychological boost that realizing those goals can bring. Wouldn't that be the cat's meow?

Your Money Blueprint:

Personal development educator, **Harv Eker**, in his book **Secrets of the Millionaire Mind** says that: "Success is a learnable skill. The fastest way for you to become and to stay rich is to work on developing YOU. Success is not a "what" but a "who"."

He asks his audiences at his Peak Potential Training Seminars: "Are you set for success, mediocrity or financial failure?" According to him, what really matters is whether you are reaching your full financial potential. Your money blueprint will determine your financial life and even your personal life. **Eke**r says that the only way to permanently change the temperature in a room is to reset the thermostat. In the same way, the only way to change your level of financial success 'permanently' is to reset your financial thermostat.

In order to reprogram your financial blueprint, you must focus on the following four elements of change:

1. Awareness: You can't change something unless you know it exists. By picking up this particular book you'll be exposed to a number of key concepts that'll heighten your awareness of what you could change or improve on a personal level.

2. Understanding: Try to understand where your ways of thinking have originated and then recognize that it has come from outside you. I'll be challenging your current ways of thinking and exposing you to several alternative approaches to creating wealth. With greater understanding, you'll be empowered to make more positive changes in your life.

3. Disassociation: Choose to either keep your beliefs or let them go – based on who you are today and where you want to be tomorrow. Whether or not you adopt all, some or none of the principles being shared in this comprehensive guide, the choice is solely up to you.

4. Reconditioning: Should you decide to embrace change for the better then read on. Learn to use the strategies in this program that generate wealth and start adopting new ways of thinking that support your happiness and success.

Eker teaches that no thought lives in your head rent-free. It is either an investment or a cost, moving you toward happiness and success or away from it. The key is to learn how to adopt beliefs that support you. In a nutshell, your thoughts lead to feelings, which in turn lead to actions, which then lead to specific results. If life is all about choices, then choosing to think and act like the rich do will move you closer to achieving your dreams. Doesn't that make sense?

Eker goes on to warn people that if you would like to be able to change your financial situation, then be willing to let go of being right and doing it your way. Why? It's because your way has gotten you exactly what you've got right now. If you want more of the same, keep doing it your way. If you want to realize your dreams then you'll need to step out of your comfort zone and grow.

Here are seven of **Eker's** top "wealth files" that'll help you change your take on money and wealth creation. Please note that when **Eker** refers to the rich or the poor he is referring to one's mentality not one's financial situation or value in society.

Wealth File #1: Rich people play the money game to win. Poor people play the money game to not lose.

Eker points out that poor people play the money game on defence, which minimizes their chances of winning. Ask yourself: Is your primary concern one of survival and security or one of creating wealth and abundance? If your goal is to be comfortable, chances are you'll never get rich. But if your goal is to be rich, chances are you'll end up mighty comfortable. Keep in mind that doing nothing is hard to do. You never know when you're done. Start taking action steps today that'll move you to where you desire.

Wealth File #2: Rich people are committed to being rich. Poor people want to be rich.

Eker believes, "The number one reason most people don't get what they want is that they don't know what they want. Rich people are totally clear that they want wealth. They are unwavering in their desire. They are fully committed to creating wealth. As long as it's legal, moral and ethical, they will do whatever it takes to have wealth. Rich people do not send mixed messages to the universe. Poor people do."

Wealth File #3: Rich people focus on opportunities. Poor people focus on obstacles.

Rich people have the mind-set 'It will work because I'll make it work.' They take educated risks, which means that they research, do their due diligence, and make decisions based on solid information and facts. When obstacles arise, they handle them and then quickly refocus on their vision. If you want to expand your wealth, focus on making, keeping, and investing your money.

Wealth File #4: Rich people admire other rich and successful people. Poor people resent rich and successful people.

In summary, **Eker** says that if you resent rich and successful people, how do you become what you despise? You should practice admiring, blessing and loving rich people. Many of us have been conditioned to think that you can't be rich and a good person or rich and spiritual. Those who are successful financially tend to be positive, reliable, hardworking, energetic, and personable.

Wealth File #5: Rich people associate with positive, successful people. Poor people associate with negative or unsuccessful people.

By learning how rich people play the money game to win and modelling their inner and outer strategies with the same mind-set, chances are that you too will become financially successful. You need to associate yourself with other positive and successful people and dissociate yourself from negative ones who drag you down. Make a point of removing yourself from toxic situations, such as: arguing, gossiping, backstabbing and mocking.

Wealth File #6: Rich people think "both". Poor people think "either/or".

Where rich people live in a world of abundance, poor people perceive their world as having limitations and not having enough to go around. By asking the question, "How can I have the benefits of both worlds (ex. career vs. family, business vs. fun, meaning in life vs. money)?" **Eker** believes that it will take you from a model of scarcity to a universe of possibilities and abundance.

Wealth File #7: Rich people act in spite of fear. Poor people let fear stop them.

Eker mentions that affirmations, meditations, and visualizations are all wonderful tools that help you to focus on becoming rich. Unfortunately, in the real world you've to take real "action" to succeed. *Eker* feels that, "fear, doubt, and worry are among the biggest obstacles, not only to success, but to happiness as well." If you want to move to a new level in your life, you must break through your comfort zone and practice doing things that are not comfortable. The only time you're actually growing is when you're uncomfortable. Training and managing your own mind is the most important skill you could ever own, in terms of both happiness and success.

The stock market offers us an arena of unlimited opportunity to accumulate wealth. The biggest limiting factor is our own belief system about money. There is a huge gap that exists between how much we believe we deserve and what is actually available from the markets should we choose to go after it.

Addressing Fear:
Let's take a closer look at how fear can hold you back from realizing your full potential as an investor.

Most fears with which you are faced every day are not real but imaginary, having been created from your thoughts and feelings. Your fears create doubt and worry, which in turn destroys your self-confidence. We all face fears. How we address our fears determines how successful we become. Unsuccessful individuals let fear stop them dead in their tracks. Let me ask you this. How do you feel about investing? Are you as nervous as a very small nun at a penguin shoot?

The negative emotions associated with fear drain energy from your body and prevent you from reaching your maximum potential. You need to turn this negative state around and learn how to identify and confront your fears head on. Fear is a powerful emotion that affects investors at all levels.

A case in point, I love kayaking. However, that love initially manifested itself in the form of fear. Despite being an excellent swimmer, I dreaded the notion of being trapped upside down in a kayak headed down the equivalent of Universal Studio's Popeye & Bluto's Bilge Rat Barges ride. If you know what I mean. Rather than give in to those fears, I decided to improve my kayaking skill level and enroll in a course that taught me how to roll my kayak when upside down. Now, I'm able to enjoy paddling in the great outdoors with greater confidence.

Learning how to address your particular fears, moves you from a point of inactivity to taking action steps that'll move you closer to your desires. Here is a simple 5-step approach to addressing your fears as an investor:

Step #1: Identify your fears.
What do you really fear the most about investing and your finances? What do you fear right now and in the future?

Many novice investors that I have spoken to have mentioned some of the following fears that are holding them back from moving forward:
- The fear of not being worthy of the riches and freedom that investing can bring.
- The fear of not being good enough to invest in anything other than what a financial advisor says.
- The fear of not knowing where to start and how to get off the ground.

Think about those fears that are holding you back from being a successful investor. What is it that is eating away at you? Take a moment to compile a list of those fears on a sheet of paper. Go ahead and do it now.

Step #2: Question your fears.

Close your eyes and visualize what would actually happen if your fears came to pass. Now ask yourself two questions: "Could I survive?" and "Could I make a comeback?" Take a moment to address each fear you've listed in this manner.

In all likelihood, the chance that you'll rise up from your failures or setbacks is very high. On a personal level, despite being scammed out of my life savings, I've discovered that no matter what my financial situation I can re-build lost wealth and achieve the lifestyle that I aspire to create.

As you can see, this reflective thinking process leads us to the next defining question: "What are the benefits to me in overcoming each fear?" Think how addressing each fear might help you achieve greater personal development and realize your dreams. List the specific benefits that'll occur from addressing and overcoming each fear. Benefits could be things like:

1. Build your confidence as an investor.
2. Be time rich.
3. Create wealth while working part-time.
4. Rebuild your lost wealth faster.
5. Generate monthly cash flow.
6. Realistically retire in 10 years or less.
7. Be at peace with your financial affairs.

You get the picture. These benefits are a strong motivator to reflect upon. When you write them down they become a tangible framework from which you can overcome any fears, apprehensions or negative thoughts. Now on to step three.

Step #3: Accept your fears.

Having identified those fears getting in the way of your success, you must now confront them. It is not necessary to try to get rid of fear in order to succeed. I repeat, it is not necessary to eliminate fear in order to succeed. Frankly, there are times when emotions get the better of me and I'm scared poopless of the actions I'm about to take.

Addressing your fears means you must move out of your comfort zone and act act in spite of fear, in spite of doubt, and even when you're NOT in the mood to act. Life is all about choices. Choose to accept and set aside your deepest fears. Decide from this point forward to act and move forward towards realizing your dreams. Everything you want in life is on the other side of your fears.

Step #4: Control your fears.

What could you do to overcome each fear? Your first task is to focus on elements you can control from within you, as opposed to elements in your external environment. You may not be able to control your current living and working conditions or the actions of others, but you can control your attitudes.

Take a moment to write down the answers to the following question: What are some elements you can control that feed your fears? Decide now to work on these specific elements and let go of external elements you're unable to control.

Step #5: Take action.

Deal with fear through massive action and positive self-talk. We create protective barriers in our mind to maintain what we have grown accustomed to, or the status quo; we avoid change. When we change our subconscious mind, it requires both time and effort before adaptation occurs. This change is in the form of reprogramming our beliefs and adopting beliefs and attitudes that support our dreams and goals in life. By making a conscious decision to change our thought process, then following up with specific actions that involve as many senses as possible, we can confront and overcome fears.

Life Change Coach **Tony Robbins** advises one to take massive action in order to better address one's fears. As he puts it, the MOTION creates EMOTION which can be re-directed to confront your fears. He suggests making pronounced physical gestures with your arms and body, moving and positioning your body in such a way that you act with confidence. By changing your posture to exude an air of confidence you begin to change your mental state from one of fear to one of certainty.

Should you have to deal with the negative emotions evoked by addressing one of your fears, try using both massive action and positive self-talk. By repeating key words and expressions that focus on positive outcomes, you can break through the fear barrier that your mind has placed in front of you. Imagine that you are talking directly to your inner sub consciousness.

Back in the day of wooden skis and bamboo poles, I competed at a national and international level in cross country skiing. Positive self-talk when the going gets tough has helped me stay focused and motivated. Try using some of the examples below that I've used with success, especially when I unconsciously allow myself to drift into negative territory. To change your negative thoughts, focus on repeating supportive ones, such as:

- I can do it! I believe in myself.
- Stay the course. Focus on my dream.
- Thank you for sharing. Now let's move on.
- Positive thoughts bring me the benefits and outcomes I desire.

- We are all faced with fear. I choose to confront my fears head on and act in spite of my fears.
- We all endure failure. When I fail, I will learn from my experience and use it to move me closer to achieving my goals.

Tony believes that the stories you tell yourself whether true or not reflect the fears that you experience. The challenge is being able to create your own new story rather than getting stuck in your old story that you keep telling yourself. This holds you back from realizing your dreams. My intent is to have you not just walk away with a certain level of enthusiasm and confidence in your abilities, but also develop specific skills that'll empower you to become a better investor. Wouldn't that be better than a poke in the eye with a sharp stick?

As *Tony* says, your success depends on three key factors. The first factor is implementing a handful of strategies. This is an easy step to initiate. It's the specific process of how you can build wealth through stock investing. The second factor is creating the right story. By changing what is negative to what is supportive, you're better capable of following through on the strategies that'll work. And the third factor is building a quality state of mind. As previously mentioned, a major focus of this particular chapter is to help you build a winning mind set.

In a nutshell, we'll look at aligning your investment strategies with your belief in yourself that is supported by a positive mind set. To help you move towards creating the positive habits and mindset that'll empower you to become a better investor, let's take a look at some focusing strategies, alright?

Focusing Strategies:
We may have good intentions of doing something that'll eventually empower us to achieve a specific desire; however, staying the

course can be a definite challenge. In the **Power of Focus**, **Jack Canfield, Mark Victor Hansen** and **Les Hewitt** share some great tips on how you can achieve your dreams. Let's take a look at some of those words of wisdom right now.

Focusing Strategy #1: Your Habits Will Determine Your Future.

Life is all about making choices, whether they be good or bad. These choices ultimately determine whether you'll live a life of abundance or one of scarcity.

Your habits are a reflection of the consistent choices that you make in life. A habit is a behaviour that you keep repeating and often becomes easier to do with time, eventually becoming a subconscious act. If you desire to change your future for the better, you must adopt both a "no exceptions" policy and consistent action to create that positive change.

More and more individuals are developing the bad habit of living for immediate gratification, without reflecting upon the negative consequences that may occur later down the road. The good news is that you can transform those negative consequences into positive rewards simply by changing your habits now.

Small adjustment to your behaviour may occur in as little as a month. The two underlying factors in determining how long it may take to change a habit are:
- How engrained or how long it has been a part of you. and
- How will rising stress levels affect you in reverting back to your old habits.

If you're unhappy with the results you're experiencing in life then you must change what you're doing. The great news is that once you've established a well-developed new habit it now becomes your normal behaviour. Keep in mind that if you keep focusing on what you've always done, you'll keep getting what you've always got.

So, how do you change bad habits? **Canfield**, **Hanson** and **Hewitt** suggest making a list of those habits that are holding you back from being the person that you would like to become. Take a good hard look at your outward behaviour. These behaviours are the true you. Focus on making adjustments quickly to these bad habits.

At this point in the book, you may wish to pause reading further and write down those bad habits that could have a negative impact on your ability to invest successfully in the stock market. When you begin to eliminate all the barriers to success, the ease at which you'll reach your objectives increases. With greater ease, your confidence level rises. And as your confidence soars, your outlook on life changes for the better.

To change bad habits, start by learning what successful people have developed as successful habits. Read their autobiographies. Watch television documentaries. Listen to audio CDs. Watch DVDs. Read books - just as you are doing right now. You're on that path to changing your life for the better.

Along with this, is the notion of replacing those behaviours that trigger a bad habit with routines that support the positive habits you would like to develop. Here's a simple example to illustrate this. If you would like to be better hydrated in the morning, set aside an empty glass in plain sight in the kitchen so that it reminds you to drink. Or if you would like to learn more about stock investing, place your book or eBook reader in a spot in your home that provides a strong visual reminder. You get the picture, right?

As simple as it may sound, continue to develop the habit of changing your bad habits. Also keep in mind that practice doesn't make perfect. Perfect practice makes perfect. Life is an on-going learning experience that never stops. Focus on striving to improve and reaching your full potential, which ultimately leads to fulfillment and prosperity.

Focusing Strategy #2: Creating Optimum Balance.
The three authors describe in detail their B-Alert system, in which each of the six letters create a well-balanced day.

B is for blueprint. Your blueprint is what you've mapped out for the day in prioritizing your tasks and recording them in your agenda. Take ten to fifteen minutes before you go to bed or early in the morning in order to plan your day. This is a great strategy to use as you learn a new set of skills, such as learning how to invest in the stock market. It's a "skookum" way to change bad habits for better ones.

A is for action. Take specific, well-planned action in those things you do best in order to produce the greatest results. Developing a quick and simple morning ritual of checking the latest financial news and how the markets are doing keeps you abreast of any developments. Spending 10 minutes in the morning could eliminate any rude awakenings that may jeopardize your positions.

L is for learning. Take time to expand your knowledge. Be curious. Learn from tapes, videos, well-selected media and books. Get into the habit of reading at least twenty minutes every day. You're on that success path right now by reading this particular book. Continue your quest to become a better well-rounded investor.

E is for exercise. Enjoy greater vitality and quality of life by getting into the habit of exercising at least twenty minutes every day. Set a thirty-day goal and have a no exceptions policy for your program. Later in this chapter, we'll talk a little about how your physical state affects the quality of your decision-making in the markets. This is not something that you see being discussed often in the stock investing arena. Yet, it can have a tremendous impact on your success as an investor.

R is for relaxation. Take time to recharge your batteries every day by taking fifteen to twenty peaceful minutes. As well, take regular breaks from your work routine to re-energize.

T is for Thinking. Spend some time at the end of your day doing some reflective thinking about what you did well, what you could improve upon and what progress you've made.

As you can surmise, each of these 6 action steps falls into the category of positive habit change. Consider focusing and working on the most problematic area of the six in developing more supportive habits.

Focusing Strategy #3: The Confidence Factor.

In the absence of confidence, fear and worry take control. What may be holding you back from resolving unfinished business is fear, which has bread doubt and this doubt has led to a loss of confidence. Businessman **George Addair's** philosophy is that everything that you desire is on the other side of fear and to overcome fear you must have faith in the outcome.

Your confidence only grows when you're willing to change and do what's necessary to move you in the direction that you desire to go. Rid yourself from the baggage of the past by learning to forgive yourself and others. When you let go and move on you, open yourself up to becoming more positive in nature.

By the time that you finish reading this book and applying the insights and skills outlined, you'll be a more confident investor. Heck, it may even trickle down into other areas of your life. Wouldn't that be awesome?

Focusing Strategy #4: Consistent Persistence.
An underlying principle of this focusing strategy is that you'll never achieve big results in your life without consistent and persistent action. You need to discover how to make consistently good choices so that you're able to realize your dreams and goals.

In order to enjoy a greater peace of mind, you need to accept total responsibility for all of your choices. Three examples of choices that'll bring you more of what you desire, are:

- To choose not to watch TV every night. Invest this time in learning more.
- To choose to not waste most of your reading time with material that'll not inspire or motivate you.
- To choose to not become a workaholic. Schedule time to develop your core relationships.

You'll notice that creating a balanced life is key to positioning yourself so that you can realize your goals. That balance encompasses your work, relationships, passions, on-going education, spirituality, fitness and mental health. Learn to consistently make good choices that'll enable you to maintain a healthy balance between all aspects of your life.

Focusing Strategy #5: Taking Decisive Action.

Are you in the habit of putting things off? The root of procrastination is lack of motivation. You've got two ways to motivate yourself, namely:

- Fearing the consequences of not taking action. or
- Being excited about the rewards or benefits of being proactive.

Here's a simple approach that may help you stay alert. It is called the TA-DA formula. The T stands for think. When faced with an important decision, take the time to reflect on all of your options. A is for ask. Ask good focusing questions of yourself that allow you to make an intelligent and informed decision. The D stands for decide. Visualize both the negative consequences of not making a decision as well as the positive benefits of moving ahead. The second A stands for act. This is the most important part of the formula. Take focused action and build momentum from your first step.

A few key points to think about in relation to money and investments are:

- Determine what money means to you. What is your current belief system around money?
- Your money habits are primarily the cause of your present financial situation. To change your habits, you must learn more about the concept of money. Make wealth a study. Does that make sense?

Investing vs. Trading:
Investor - Trader - Speculator - Gambler. Which one are you?

Scott Kyle in his book ***The Power Curve*** talks about the differences between investing and trading. He points out that: "Trading is associated with risk-taking and with gambling, but I believe that speculation and gambling are functions not of time frames but mind-sets and one's knowledge basis."

I tend to concur. It is not the activity that defines whether it is gambling or investing, it is the ability of the educated investor to consistently generate returns that factors in as to whether that activity will be speculative or not.

I think of investing as allocating capital with a time horizon of a year or more with the objective of gaining a return on that money in the form of capital appreciation of the stock price and through cash flow from dividends and options. Trading would be defined as allocating capital with a time frame of less than one year with the goal of generating the same types of returns. It may help to think of your trading and investing opportunities as falling within a time continuum extending from just a few days to several years.

The main purpose of the accelerated cash flow system you're being shown is to generate consistent profits over time that arises from:
1. Capital appreciation of your stock price.
2. Income from dividends. and
3. Income from covered call option sales.

So how does passive vs. active investing fit into this context?

The Passive vs. Active Investor/ Trader:
A passive investor believes that the markets are generally efficient in generating a return on their investment. The passive investor is willing to accept market returns in exchange for little involvement in the process. Most individuals who have their money parked in mutual funds fall into this category. They typically pay hefty management fees to have someone else manage their holdings.

These fees can be substantial and erode your capital appreciation over time. For example, if your mutual fund provides you with an 8% annual return and management fees account for 2%, you're giving up 25% of your potential growth for the convenience of having someone else look after your investments. Not only that, but your broker gets paid no matter what, whether the stocks in the fund go up or down. More about this a bit later in the book.

An active investor believes that the markets are not efficient and that he or she can actively be involved in the process of buying and selling positions thus achieving above average returns. This is the basis of this resource - empowering you to become a better more confident active investor.

Note that you can make money investing, you can make money trading, you can make money being passive, and you can make money being active. These are the choices that every investor has to make at some point in time. When you commit the necessary time to learn how to generate profits in the stock market by actively investing under any market conditions, you'll be light years ahead of the majority of individuals using the traditional buy and pray the stock goes up passive approach.

Kyle goes on to say that: "While most people think of Warren Buffett as a buy-and-hold only investor, and the typical view of Jim Cramer is that he is a lightning fast trader, these two men are not far apart in terms of style as it would appear. Buffett is constantly getting in and out of positions, be they equities or special situations, from commodities to currencies, to everything in between. Similarly, while Cramer is undoubtedly more active than Buffett in terms of equity holdings, he maintains many positions for years, as long as the fundamentals stay strong. Simply put, the very best money managers are both investors and traders, and they know which hat they are wearing at any point in time and, more importantly, why."

In this book, you may hear me using the terms investor and trader interchangeably, since we are both investors and traders depending on the context of the situation. The key is to know in advance whether capital is being allocated for an investment or a trade. You can make money both ways, especially if trading is effectively combined with investing. However, each situation requires a different mindset and approach in order to maximize your potential gains and minimize your risks. Which brings us to …

The Dangers of Day Trading:

Janet Lowe in her book *The Triumph of Value Investing* cautions investors about the dangers of day trading. She says that: "There are hundreds of organizations appealing to the gambling instinct in most of us by marketing the idea that you can sit at home all day in your pajamas and earn a fabulous living as a day trader. The pitchmen are making great money providing training, software, and support, which in some cases can cost as much as $45.000."

Several studies have shown that approximately 70% of day traders lose money and are wiped out within the first year of trading. This program does NOT teach you how to become a day trader.

A fundamental question to keep in the back of your mind as you begin investing is am I investing or gambling with my money? Some of the tell-tale signs of individuals who believe that they are investing but actually are gambling are that they:
- Engage in speculative risk taking resulting in significant losses in relation to their level of assets.
- Chase losses through increasing speculation or have difficulty in stopping when they are losing.
- Borrow excessive amounts of money in order to "invest."

- Display erratic, inconsistent, or irrational trading behavior.
- Place trades too frequently.

Here are five guidelines to follow when any of these signs appears:

1. Never use money set aside for your daily living expenses. Although saving and investing should be your number one household priority, this comes after you've met your basic needs of shelter and food.
2. Always set a dollar limit on the amount of money you can "afford" to lose in the markets. When that amount of money is gone, stop making trades until you re-build your capital base through saving. The amount of capital loss should never be greater than 30-50% of your total portfolio.
3. Avoid chasing your losses by increasing your trading. You increase the risk of losing more money. Sit back, re-group and re-think what you could specifically do to improve your performance. By sitting on the sidelines you'll be able to re-assess how you can better play the mental game of investing.
4. Systematically take some of your profits off the table and move them into longer time horizon investments that can provide you with a greater level of safety of capital.
5. Shift your capital allocation so that more of your hard-earned dollars are targeted for purchasing stock of those market leaders who are best of breed in their industry.

Developing Your Winning Edge:

According to **Mark Douglas** in **Trading in the Zone**: "The goal of any trader is to turn consistent profits on a regular basis, yet so few people ever really make consistent money as traders. What accounts for the small percentage of traders who are consistently successful? To me, the determining factor is psychological - consistent winners think differently from everyone else."

If **Douglas** believes that success depends on your mental attitude then it stands to reason that by learning how to change your mind set, you can learn how to create consistent profits in the stock market as an investor.

Douglas goes on to say that: "The defining characteristic that separates the consistent winners from everyone else is this: The winners have attained a mind-set - a unique set of attitudes - that allows them to remain disciplined, focused, and, above all, confident in spite of the adverse conditions. As a result, they are no longer susceptible to the common fears and trading errors that plague everyone else."

A perfect example to illustrate this notion is the precipitous drop in stock price of The Dollar Tree in March 2018. Had you just invested in the stock, you would have had to wait until Mr. Market brought the stock price back up to your breakeven point. On the flip side, had you sold an option contract when you had invested in The Dollar Tree you could have continued generating monthly or bi-monthly premiums that'll get you back to even faster. Which approach makes better sense to you?

When you realize that the stock market goes through hissy fits every once in a while, you can better navigate the ups and downs by knowing how to generate cash flow despite your stock having been hammered. Theoretically, you could continue to see option premiums being deposited into your trading account on a consistent basis even though the book (paper) value of your stock is down. Having the confidence to not panic and pull the plug on your stock, thereby creating a loss comes with developing that winning mindset. You haven't lost any hard-earned capital until you sell your stock for a "realized" loss. If the company is still a market leader, eventually the stock price will trend higher over time. It's your state of mind, your specific beliefs and attitude that'll determine your results. To build a winner's mindset you need to think more in terms of probabilities.

Winning in any endeavor is mostly a function of attitude. Investing is no different. Many novice investors experience the feeling of a winning attitude since they are very often not operating out of fear. This does not mean that they have a winning attitude, only that they have yet to experience the pain of losing from investing and the resulting fear that ensues. Losing and being wrong are part of the game of investing. Once you learn how to accept loss as a normal part of your investing, you better position yourself mentally to get back into the game and looking forward to the next opportunity.

Hopefully, by tapping into the wealth of knowledge contained in this resource you'll be empowered with insights and tips that'll minimize any potential future losses. Wouldn't that be better than a kick in the pants?

Three Fundamental Truths about Investing:
The three fundamental truths to come to grips with in order to gain a consistent edge when investing are:
Truth #1: Anything can happen in the markets.
Stock prices go up and they go down. There may be no logical explanation other than that the markets are frequented by emotionally charged traders with real fears and occasional allusions of grandeur or invincibility. Be prepared emotionally to handle this truth by entering each position with a neutral realistic expectation. Avoid getting caught up in the emotional hype of the market. Base your decision-making process first on sound rational reasoning, then on assessing what other investors may be thinking and feeling. Are they panicking, elated, fearful, etc.?

***Truth #2: An edge is just a higher probability of one
thing happening over another.***

Having an edge is not based on hope or being obsessed with
gathering evidence to support your position. Base each
investment decision only on the specific variables that you use to
pre-define your edge in determining if your next trade has a higher
probability of working out in your favor.

Truth #3: Every opportunity in the market is unique.

Don't set yourself up for disappointment by trying to correctly
predict what the market will do next. Open your mind up to the
possibility of what the market is offering you from the perspective
of each investment opportunity being unique and is therefore not
based on previous patterns or trends. Although past success can
be a great predictor of future success, the markets never trend
higher by following a straight line. They snake their way up. By
accepting this truth, you can mentally stay the course, especially
once you know how to use some of the entry and exit strategies
outlined in this book.

Hopefully, by accepting these three fundamental truths about
investing, you'll learn to accept the risks in such a way that you
begin to eliminate interpreting market information in painful ways
that could cloud your future judgment. Does that sound good?

Accepting Risk:

All stock investments are inherently risky because the outcomes
are probable - not guaranteed. They are based on the probability
of success. Unfortunately, there are no guarantees of success.
Learning to accept this risk is the most important investing skill.
Many investors fail to realize this fundamental truth, especially
those who plunk their money into mutual funds.

Great traders are able to move into positions without the slightest bit of hesitation or internal conflict. They can get out of a losing position and doing so doesn't evoke the slightest bit of emotional discomfort. In other words, the risks that are a part of all investing do not cause the great investors to lose their discipline, focus, or sense of confidence.

Douglas poses this fundamental question: "How do we remain disciplined, focused and confident in the face of constant uncertainty? When you've learned how to think like a trader, that's exactly what you'll be able to do. Learning how to redefine your trading activities in a way that allows you to completely accept the risk is the key to thinking like a successful trader. Learning to accept the risk is a trading skill - the most important skill you can learn. Yet it's rare that developing traders focus any attention or expend any effort to learn it."

Great investors aren't afraid to act. They aren't afraid because they have developed attitudes that give them the greatest mental flexibility to flow in and out of the market. This is based on what the market is telling them about the possibilities from its perspective. Great investors have also developed attitudes that prevent them from getting reckless.

The vast majority of the trading errors you're likely to make that cause your money to just evaporate before your eyes will arise from four primary trading fears. These four fears are:
1. Being wrong.
2. Losing money.
3. Missing out.
4. Leaving money on the table.

Keep in mind that trading has no formal ending. The market will not take you out of a trade. You can become a passive loser. This means that you can simply ignore the situation and the market will take everything that you own. You must develop a pre-defined plan to end each and every trade in a manner that is always in your best interest. This is why I spend so much time in the coming chapters exploring entry and exit strategies for your positions. When you're armed with an arsenal of tools to choose from, your confidence soars to new heights. Wouldn't that be enlightening?

What's the solution?
Learn how to adjust your attitudes and beliefs about investing and trading in such a way that you can move in and out of opportunities without the slightest bit of fear while having a system in place that does not allow you to become reckless. So how do you actually go about doing this? Let's explore the following four action plans:
1. Follow pre-defined rules.
2. Take full responsibility
3. Be consistent.
4. Train your mind.

Action Step #1: Follow Pre-Defined Rules.
Start by creating a system of rules that define specifically at what point you'll both exit and enter an opportunity based on likely outcomes or probabilities. Then, stick to those rules when an investment triggers a course of action to take as the market moves either in one direction or another.

Here are the top 12 basic rules that many of the investment industry's respected experts suggest that you consider as part of your overall investment plan:
1. Own the best of breed; it's worth it. When the choice is among two or three companies in an industry, always go for the industry leader regardless of the price.
2. If you want to build a sizeable position over time, buy in increments. Don't buy all at once. Always keep a small portion of your regular contributions in cash for those market breaks.

3. It is impossible to own more than 20 stocks unless you are a full-time stock junkie. The right-sized diversified portfolio where you can do it yourself is between 5 and 10 stocks.

4. Sitting in cash on the sidelines may be a fine alternative. When the market is overvalued, take stock off, raise cash and get ready for the next decline. Sell strength and buy weakness in the stocks of companies you love and understand.

5. Buy stocks that you believe should go higher because of the fundamentals and avoid stocks where the underlying business is bad or getting worse. Also, monitor those companies that have unfairly been beaten up despite solid fundamentals. They may provide great growth opportunities.

6. Take your profits off the table. Keep in mind that you don't have a profit until you sell. You should not confuse book gains with real gains. Those gains not taken can turn out to be losses down the road. Always take profits rather than worry about paying taxes and losing out on an opportunity entirely.

7. Take excessive emotional mood swings out of investing. Stick to your process of investing. A patient, less panicked style of investing always generates a higher return.

8. Be flexible and open to change. Something good one month can turn bad. Stay on top of monitoring each position.

9. Just because someone says it on TV doesn't make it so. Don't trust anything you hear. Do your own due diligence. If you like it and understand it, then buy it.

10. Cut your losses quickly. It's okay to take a loss when you already have one. A loss is a loss whether realized or unrealized. By controlling your losses, you can let your winners do the running.

11. Don't buy or sell stock on any tip. All of your trades require that you do your due diligence to verify if the opportunity merits action on your part. Remember, tips are for waiters, not for traders.

12. Be patient. Sometimes a stock on your watch list that you like does nothing for ages. Many turnarounds take 12 - 18 months before the business takes off. Eventually, these stocks, especially if they are undervalued, rise up to their true intrinsic value.

Action Step #2: Take Full Responsibility.

The second step is to take full responsibility for your actions or lack thereof. You must start with the premise that no matter what the outcome of a particular investment decision, you're completely responsible. No need to blame yourself, Mr. Market, your online broker or your pet hamster for your results. Yes, learn from any errors that you've made. However, don't dwell on the negative outcome. Keep in mind that each and every potential investment presents itself as a unique opportunity. The answer is to re-focus your time and energy on the next potential opportunity.

From the market's perspective, each moment is neutral having no meaning. It cares not whether each opportunity being presented leads to a gain or a loss. On the other hand, many investors try to attach meaning to market moves, leading to interpreting information in a negative emotional manner. When you perceive the market as an endless stream of opportunities to enter and exit trades without beating yourself up when negative outcomes arise, you'll be in the best position to create that consistent winning attitude.

By setting aside negative emotions associated with investing, you free your mind up to focus on moving into and out of better and better opportunities in the market. Now, isn't that what we're trying to accomplish?

Action Step #3: Be Consistent.

Being consistent should be a natural expression of who you are as an investor. There should be no effort or struggle in trying to "be" consistent with your results. You should see opportunities unfold before you and your actions should appear effortless with no emotional struggle or resistance.

Mark Douglas believes that: "what separates the best traders from everyone else, is not what they do or when they do it, but rather how they think about what they do and how they're thinking when they do it."

If your goal is to eventually invest like a professional then you must start from the premise that the solutions are in your mind and not in the market. Consistency is a state of mind.

Douglas's Seven Principles of Consistency:
Worth including in this chapter are seven principles for becoming a more consistent winner. This should help you better develop your winning edge. And here they are:
1. I objectively identify my edges.
2. I predefine the risk of every trade.
3. I completely accept the risk or I am willing to let go of the trade.
4. I act on my edges without reservation or hesitation.
5. I pay myself as the market makes money available to me.
6. I continually monitor my susceptibility for making errors.
7. I understand the absolute necessity of these principles of consistent success and, therefore, I never violate them.

To become the investor that you've always wanted to become, requires that you make up your mind with as much conviction and clarity as possible, that more than anything else you desire consistency from your investing. In doing so, you'll begin to create the state of mind of trust, confidence and objectivity.

To be able to realize consistency in your investing requires that you:

- Have developed an "edge" that puts the odds of success in your favor.
- Think about trading in the appropriate manner based on the three fundamental truths mentioned previously.
- Act in a manner that allows you to put on a series of trades over time.

Now, at this point you may be asking yourself: "Hey Randall, enough of your sermon, how do I develop my edge?" In a nutshell, to arrive at your edge, you'll need to choose a set of market variables whether they be mathematical, mechanical or visual, which we'll cover in part two of this book. These variables need to be precise so that you can enter the market at a specific point in time based solely an objective decision-making process. You should not have to make any subjective decisions based on an emotional decision-making process. If the market meets your strict criteria you've got a trade; otherwise, you don't. Make sense so far?

The same objectivity applies to exiting your trade. You must predefine the exact amount of money you need to risk to find out if the trade is going to work. Your exit point should require no subjective decision making. We'll delve deeper into the specifics of entering and exiting positions later.

Action Step #4: Train Your Mind,

As **Douglas** says: "The market does not generate happy or painful information. From the market's perspective, it's all simply information. It may seem as if the market is causing you to feel the way you do at any given moment, but that's not the case. It's your own mental framework that determines how you perceive the information, how you feel, and, as a result, whether or not you're in the most conducive state of mind to spontaneously enter the flow and take advantage of whatever the market is offering."

Your goal is to train your mind so that you don't perceive anything about the markets as being painful. In doing so, no threat exists and there is no need for you to react in a defensive manner. You must look at the markets from an objective point of view, devoid of extreme negative emotions or the effects of overconfidence or euphoria.

 The secret nature of investing is that at the very core of one's ability, you should:
- Trade without fear or overconfidence.
- Perceive what the market is offering from its perspective.
- Stay completely focused in the "now moment opportunity flow".
- Spontaneously enter the "zone", which is a strong virtually unshakeable belief in an uncertain outcome with an edge in your favor.

Knowing, Not Controlling, Your Emotions is the Key to Successful Investing:

Many stock investing experts talk about taking the emotional side out of your decision-making when investing. They recommend that you leave your emotions at the door step and focus on a rational approach to arriving at each trading decision. This is based on a sound analysis of the business's fundamentals, coupled with a thorough analysis of the technical indicators.

This common advice does bear some weight as a sound approach when moving into and out of the markets. All investors should try to maintain a level head when making decisions and not get caught up in emotional extremes of euphoria or panic.

Avoid Controlling Your Emotions.

However, recent neuroscience research suggests that using our emotions to INFORM us rather than trying to control our emotions actually reduces risky decision-making.

Denise Shull in her ground-breaking book, *Market Mind Games*, which delves into investment decision psychology, quotes a recent scientific study in saying that: "Contrary to the popular belief that feelings are generally bad for decision making, we found that individuals who experienced more intense feelings had higher decision-making performance…" This was followed by another equally important quote: "Individuals who were better able to identify and distinguish among their current feelings achieved higher decision-making performance…"

If all judgment requires emotion, then it stands to reason that treating our feelings as data provide us with another input signal to guide our decision-making ability. It is ironic that we like feelings to arise when we are involved in any kind performance activity such as sports, yet we're told to avoid allowing our feelings to interfere with our investment decisions.

Shull goes on to say that: "Every day research proves that not only are emotions not something to be shunned, dismissed, or overridden, but we need them for meaning, we need them for vision, and we use them for essentially everything."

So, if emotions are best factored into our investment decision-making process, then what should we be focusing on?

Here are 3 action steps that you can take, which will empower you to become a better investor:

Action Step #1: Learn to anticipate, notice and name your different combinations of feelings when you place any trades.

The first order of business is to anticipate that your body is going to react in a certain way to an investment decision or trade. The next step is to notice which feelings come to the forefront. Finally, take a moment to name that feeling and document this information in a journal or trading diary of some sort. I quickly jot down this info in my daily planner. It helps me reflect upon past situations and positions that I took in the market. Something worth considering, right?

The five most common categories of feelings associated with investing are anger, fear, disgust, sadness and pleasure. These feelings can be plotted along a fear spectrum, with the fear of losing at one extreme along a horizontal line and the fear of missing out at the other end. The middle ground would represent the emotions of pleasure or contentment.

The more conscious you're aware of specific feelings, the sooner you can use this knowledge about yourself in risk management. Your future goal now becomes shifting your emotional energy towards the middle ground of pleasure or contentment where you know you're going to make more confident decisions.

Your investment process should take into account three important sources of information:

- The fundamental analysis of the stock - those key ratios that define the stock as being a market leader and best of breed within its sector or industry.
- The technical analysis of the stock, which identifies how investor sentiment, market momentum and market trend come into play in assessing the growth potential of the opportunity.

- The mental analysis of the trade. How is your emotional state of mind as you enter the trade and your winning edge going to possibly play out for you?

As you gather information about a particular trade, your level of certainty about the key factors that'll influence a stock's price movement will become that much clearer. With increased clarity, you're now developing a stronger "edge" that increases your probability of success. Put another way, it is the combination of your rational assessment of the opportunity, coupled with your understanding of your current mental mind-set that gives you an edge which increases your probability of success in the markets.

Your knowledge of how this fear spectrum works in the world of investing allows you to use this tool to read others in the marketplace. They too live on this spectrum as well. That in essence is a critical step to developing your winning edge when you place your trades. On a personal level, it was my major breakthrough in understanding how I can use panic or greed in the market to my advantage. Market volatility can be your friend when you know how to use it to your benefit.

Let's take a quick look at how this can help you, which brings us to action step #2.

Action Step #2: Learn to think about how the future will play out in the other investor's minds.
You'll make more money by correctly predicting the other traders' future perception of what is going to play out in the market and not base your trades on facts alone.

Facts do have an important place when placing any trades. However, you must use the facts in the proper context as the underlying basis for your investment decision. Now you must look at each investment opportunity from a social context. That is to say, how do you think other investors are going to value the stock in question differently in the future? By thinking "socially" you put yourself into the right frame of mind to make the best judgment calls.

Finally, if you want to take your investing to a new level, I strongly encourage you to consider your investing from a physical perspective.

Action Step #3: Look at trading as a physical game.
As **Denise Shull** points out: "We tend to think our market asset is limited to our cash capital. We also tend to think only of our intellectual capacities as the avenue to an edge. In both cases, we omit a key factor in our success - our total mental or psychological capital. Think of "psyche cap" as the sum total of your physical, mental and emotional energy available to you at any one time."

Your psyche cap varies day to day depending on numerous factors that are affecting your life at any one given moment. It stands to reason that you should not trade when you're sick or tired since your psyche cap will be at a low level thus potentially affecting your edge in the markets. Trading when you're under the weather can have a disastrous effect on your investment portfolio - you'll probably lose money.

As well, by improving your physical state of being, this in turn improves your mental ability, which in turn improves' your ability to read the market, which improves your overall results. Wow! That was a mouthful.

Just like an athlete performs better when in shape, you too will perform better in the markets when you take better care of your body and mind. Taking the time to "read" your physical, mental and emotional states when you enter and exit the markets will give you that extra edge that'll translate into higher more consistent returns over time.

Top 5 Pitfalls to Investing and Trading:
The following are the top five pitfalls to investing that set back many a novice investor according to some of the top investment educators in the market today:

Pitfall #1: Ignoring the learning curve.
It is critical to your long-term success as an investor to work on your weaknesses while playing to your strengths. It takes time to develop an investor-trader mindset that'll serve you well in any type of market environment. With patience and perseverance, you'll eventually achieve your core desires that are motivating you to become a cash flow investor. Take the time to gain the knowledge first, then the experience. As well, learn from your mistakes don't just dismiss them without analyzing the why behind the error.

Pitfall #2: Lacking formal training.
Robert Kiyosaki in his book **Rich Dad's Guide to Investing** says that if you think of time as being precious and that it has a price, the richer you'll become. The poor measure in money and the rich measure in time. If you desire to be rich you need to invest in something more valuable than money, time in learning and studying about investment.

As you learn new skills your financial IQ increases. By taking the time to learn how to use multiple strategies in building your wealth, you quickly build your confidence, which will serve you well for decades down the road. How much better would that be? Focus on becoming a consummate learner and keep an open mind to learning new concepts and approaches.

Pitfall #3: Expecting radical success and huge profits too soon.

Unfortunately, the internet is full of get rich quick schemes that promise riches beyond your wildest dreams in unrealistic time frames and with incredible risk to your hard-earned capital.

With any initial venture, it's important to set realistic expectations and look for smaller returns to start. By keeping your goals modest in the beginning and taking baby steps, your ability to succeed over time increases dramatically. Start by putting in your time learning and gaining experience. The market is going nowhere. There will always be great opportunities for you to realize significant profits over time.

Pitfall #4: Overtrading and risking too much.

Your primary objective has to be to preserve your precious capital. This means that you cannot afford to take on too much risk or chase the market for higher returns. This pitfall often stems from a lack of patience with your progress. The stark reality is that it will require effort on your part to change who you are as an investor so that you can effortlessly move into and out of opportunities without increased risk or over exposure. As well, we all learn at different rates. There is no point in trying to rush the transformational process at the expense of your capital.

Pitfall #5: Lack of consistency and increased frustration.

Investing is simply a plan and a system, made up of formulas and strategies that allow you to become wealthy. If a formula is overly complex, it's not worth following. If you're following too many strategies at once, you'll probably abandon your efforts out of sheer frustration.

Consistent Investing involves these 3 steps:
- Preparation - which is doing your research and due diligence on every investment opportunity.
- Planning - what approach and strategies you'll use to enter and exit your positions.
- Pre-commitment - to a specific investment strategy when in a rational state of mind.

Keep in mind that optimism or hope is not a good investment strategy. You need to plan in advance how you'll anticipate entering and exiting your positions so that you can optimize your returns. More on this in Chapter 4.

Your Growth as an Investor:
The successful investor that you want to become is just a future projection of yourself that you've grown into over a period of time. This period of growth means that you must move outside of your comfort zone and challenge your current beliefs and attitudes as you learn how to become the investor that you've always dreamt of becoming.

As you can now see, what separates the average investor from great investors is not one's ability to analyze a company's fundamentals or read technical charts, it is the mental game associated with investing.

The purpose of this initial module was to provide you with a simple mental framework that empowers you to achieve your financial dreams sooner than later. And your attitude has a lot to do with your ability to achieve what you desire in life and ultimately your overall success. Here are six confidence-building strategies to help you develop and maintain a positive attitude:
1. Remind yourself every day that you did something well.
2. Read inspiring autobiographies and biographies.
3. Be thankful or grateful for what you have in your life.

4. Build excellent support around yourself through your fortress of family members, close friends, trusted colleagues and committed professionals.
5. Push yourself to accomplish your short-term goals (like getting through this book).
6. Celebrate your weekly accomplishments. Learn to applaud them.

What is the price of becoming well-off? The cost of you becoming financially free is that it requires time and dedication in order to gain the education, experience, and cash to safely invest in the markets. Let's explore how you can begin creating the life of your dreams in the next chapter that outlines the specific framework from which to build your wealth.

Chapter 3 - Getting a Grip on Money Management

Focus Questions:
1. How do self-made millionaires manage their financial affairs?
2. What does my household money management plan look like?
3. How could I be saving more for investing?
4. How do I make the best of my 401(k) or IRA investment accounts [RRSP & TFSA in Canada]?
5. How do I avoid being scammed in any investment opportunity?

This chapter will provide you with a step-by-step process to better manage your finances so that you're able to generate wealth at an accelerated pace and achieve your dreams that much sooner.

By learning how you can better allocate your financial resources to those priorities that will make an actual difference to building wealth, you'll empower yourself to achieve those goals you've set out for yourself when it comes to investing.

My overall intention with this particular chapter is to decrease the stress that financial hardship can bring on you and your family members by providing you with some tools and helpful advice. This will allow you to move in the right direction with your money matters.

With a few money management strategies under your belt, you'll stop worrying about struggling to pay your bills. Then, you'll be able to focus your time and energy on realizing your dreams. Let's dive right into this chapter and take a quick look at how the rich think about their finances and investing. Alright?

Robert Kiyosaki in his book *Rich Dad's Guide to Investing* so aptly put it by saying that: "When it comes to money and investing, people have three fundamental reasons or choices for investing. They are:

- To be secure.
- To be comfortable. or
- To be rich."

He goes on to point out that: "For most people, if becoming rich disturbs their comfort or makes them feel insecure, they will forsake becoming rich. That is why so many people want that one hot investment tip. People who make security and comfort their first and second choices look for ways to get rich quick that are easy, risk free, and comfortable. A few people do get rich on one lucky investment, but all too often they lose it all again."

Before beginning to invest, you need to decide what your priorities are going to be. If your core desire is focused on wealth building so that you can provide a better life for you and your family, then by developing more financial skills you'll be able to create more abundance in your life. Let's start by finding out how self-made millionaires have managed their financial affairs.

How Millionaires Manage Their Financial Affairs:
In *Stanley* and *Danko's* revealing book *The Millionaire Next Door*, they share 7 key characteristics of self-made millionaires. The authors make it perfectly clear how you can attain millionaire status by changing how you think about wealth creation. By changing your attitude about saving and investing, you can change your destiny.

Here is a summary of their key findings:
1. All self-made millionaires live below their means, but within their needs. They choose to build wealth rather than

succumb to the instant gratification that comes with being a typical North American consumer.

2. They allocate both their time and monetary resources efficiently in order to build sustainable wealth.
3. They believe that financial independence is more important than displaying their social status with the latest Armani suit, Rolex watch or BMW car.
4. The vast majority of self-made millionaires did not receive any economic "out-patient care" from their parents. In other words, they did not receive any significant financial gifts to get them where they are.
5. The children of self-made millionaires are economically self-sufficient. This aligns well with the above point.
6. Self-made millionaires are proficient in targeting investment opportunities. They take an active role in their financial and investment decisions. A fundamental goal of this book is to show you how you can be more effective in targeting opportunities in the wonderful world of stock investing.
7. They have chosen the right occupation that allows them the opportunity to better amass wealth. Many self-made millionaires are successful business entrepreneurs with a college education.

So, if the overwhelming majority of self-made millionaires of America are not high paid surgeons, lawyers or corporate executives who are they then? The simple answer is to look no further than your neighbor down the street with the middle-class lifestyle.

Stanley and **Danko** point out in their findings that to become wealthy requires focusing primarily on three factors, namely:
- Discipline - staying with a simple wealth accumulation plan.

- Self-sacrifice - placing more importance on realizing one's dreams as opposed to paying for one's high-priced lifestyle and immediate desires.
- Hard work - realizing that wealth building is an active process requiring ongoing effort.

The big question to ask yourself is: Am I willing to re-orient my lifestyle today and make the necessary sacrifices to become wealthier?

Five Steps to Better Money Management:
Your financial success can be boiled down to the answer you give to one question: "How well do I manage my money?" Begin today to take better control of your financial affairs. Create the positive habit of effectively managing your money, no matter how much you start with. Here are those five steps for taking better control of your affairs:

Step #1: Involve your whole family in the learning process.
Engage your whole family in learning about how to effectively manage money. Don't keep your financial affairs or investments a secret. If you truly believe that your life purpose is to add value to other people's lives, then include all your family members in learning about finances.

Could you have your children get involved in helping you pick stocks? Sure you could, especially if they're looking at familiar brands like Disney, Netflix and Apple.

Ongoing communication about your financial matters is an absolute must if you would like to establish trust, security, individual accountability and a sense of financial peace within your household. In order to facilitate the process, I encourage you to develop a few basic skills in active listening that will encourage dialog and commitment to a core family value.

Develop the Skill of Active Listening:
The key to following through on having money management become a core family value is to focus on active listening when discussing financial matters with your spouse or family members.

Active listening involves focusing your attention on what the other person is saying without interrupting or being judgmental. This means allowing the individual time to express his or her thoughts, concerns, fears and insights.

You want to avoid erecting barriers that get in the way of you hearing what is being said. As well, avoid over-reacting to highly charged or emotional words. In other words, hear the person out.

As you actively listen to someone, try to observe his or her body language for clues as to their feelings and true thoughts. Express your understanding with positive words and by paraphrasing for clarification. Paraphrasing is restating a comment made by someone. Start by asking reflective questions (i.e. how, why, when, where, what, who) in an attempt to draw more specific information out of the conversation. Make every effort to concentrate on what is being said. Actively try to hear every word.

Your ability to connect with someone is directly related to how approachable you are. Active listening is something that we do out of caring and concern for others. Show a genuine interest in what they have to say. Seek to clarify and understand. Try to leave each individual feeling better for having talked to you and for having shared his or her concerns and thoughts.

I would suggest that within the next couple of weeks that you arrange a financial date with your spouse, accountability partner or a mentor. Block out enough time to ensure you can discuss your most pressing financial matters openly without distractions or time pressures. Your goal should be to review the specific details of your financial records, reports, policies and cash flow to gain an in-depth understanding of where you are. Before you're able to change how you manage your money, you need to know what potential areas could be improved. Does that make sense?

Step #2: Reduce your debt load and expenses while increasing your savings.

Is your wallet like an onion? When you open it up, does it make you cry? Could you decrease your expenditures and be content with getting by with a little less? Take a moment to list three to five areas you could cut back on right away that would allow you to reallocate the money not spent to increase your savings over time.

Reducing your debt load may be a long-term goal, but once you eliminate the heavy burden of bad debt, you can begin accumulating wealth. As a general rule, attempt to save ten percent of your net earnings every month. You may need to build up to this level of contribution slowly, as you also work towards reducing your debt.

Make saving a priority in your life and the lives of your family members. Once your savings begin to accumulate, move them out of low interest-bearing accounts and invest in high interest-bearing or cash flow financial instruments like the ones we'll be using in this book.

As *MJ DeMarco* points out in his book *The Millionaire Fastlane*: "Live below your means with the intent to expand your means." Although you want to keep expenses under control, you do want to foster a saving and investing regime that'll move you closer to achieving your financial goals.

Step #3: Gain peace of mind with your emergency fund.

There is nothing like being worry free of knowing how you'll pay for the next crisis down the road. Your goal should be to build up enough reserve funds over the course of the next year to cover at least two to three months of your normal expenses.

Start by opening a savings account or money market account that doesn't penalize you for deposits and withdrawals. Initially, call this your emergency account, which is used to buffer your expenses when unexpected events happen. Eventually, you'll also be able to set aside savings for long-term projects such as dream vacations, post-secondary education or major projects around the home.

I personally directed a good portion of my savings into acquiring precious metals during the boom at the turn of the century rather than keeping it in a low interest-bearing account or money market fund. Then, when the precious metals boom started to wane, I moved these funds into the stock market selecting an Exchange Traded Fund that mirrored the S&P 500. Both strategies proved to be winners.

Step #4: Create balance in your money management plan.

The following money management plan was one that I picked up from **Harv Eker** at a **Millionaire Intensive** Weekend Seminar. It allows you to build up your savings and rewards you every month for your efforts.

He suggests that you begin by setting up separate accounts within your main banking account for each of the following categories and allocate funds in accordance with the recommended amounts:

10% of your net income for investing in your financial freedom

Imagine that you have just acquired two or three "financial freedom goslings." These are no ordinary goslings, but ones that eventually produce golden eggs. Your responsibility is to feed your little golden geese every month, building up your capital in various investments, such as stocks, real estate, commodities, and systematized businesses.

Eventually you'll be able to use the golden eggs, which is the accumulation of the cash flow and interest earned from your investments, to support your desired lifestyle. At no point in time should you kill any golden goose by spending the capital that you have already invested. You may reallocate capital to finance a project that is going to create wealth, but avoid the temptation to pay off any expenses by killing a goose.

10% for play

Life should be enjoyed now and through retirement. A secret to managing money well is establishing balance between hard work and rewarding yourself. Your play account should be spent each month on ways that rejuvenate your body and spirit such as a weekend getaway for two, a meal in a classy restaurant or a day at a health spa.

Get into the habit of doing something that'll create a lasting memory which will keep you motivated and focused until the next month's memorable moment. Treating yourself on a monthly basis helps with your mental game, not to mention making it easier to stay motivated and focused on pursuing wealth.

10% for your education
Your financial literacy is fundamental to becoming a wise investor. Many people believe that certain types of investments are very risky. It is not the investment vehicle that is too risky; it is the unknowing investor.

In order to reduce your risk, you need to develop good financial and business knowledge and skills. Your goal is to learn how to convert earned income into several relatively passive income streams.

This knowledge may be gained from a variety of sources, such as home self-study courses, workshops, seminars, conferences, books, magazines, CDs, websites and investment clubs. You get the picture, right?

I personally spend a good portion of my monthly education allocation on audio and books. The combination of the two allows me to tap into different learning styles. You may wish to explore different ways of tapping into the wealth of investment knowledge out there by adopting a similar approach.

10% for your emergency fund and future projects
As already mentioned, try to set aside money to cover any unforeseen expenses in order to give yourself a better sense of peace of mind.

Once you're able to set aside the equivalent of two to three months of expenses, you'll then be in a position to save for long-term projects. These longer-term projects or what I call saving for sunny day events, as opposed to rainy day events, will help keep you motivated over the long haul.

10% for giving
Giving not only brings joy to others; it also brings you a sense of gratification in knowing that you are adding value to other people's lives.

Get into the habit of supporting your community and helping those in need by giving a portion of your earnings away on a regular basis to a worthy cause. Give freely from your heart and not out of a sense of obligation. The simple act of buying the homeless a decent meal goes a long way in rejuvenating your soul and connecting to a higher purpose.

50% for necessities
The majority of your monthly financial obligations or expenses fall into this category. Make a concerted effort to reduce your expenses in the early goings by cutting back on certain luxuries or desires that seem to crop up on a daily or weekly basis. Do you really need to spend a few bucks each day on specialty coffees? Ya, once in a while is a nice treat. Who doesn't like to be treated? But when it becomes a habit that reduces your saving for investing potential, then this one choice could have a long-term negative impact on the direction you would like to see your life head in.

The first key factor to getting ahead is coming to an agreement with your spouse about how you'll manage your financial affairs, including your long-term financial goals. The second key factor is in slowly reducing both your debt load and expenses while increasing savings for purchasing various investments. Be patient with the process. It takes time to fatten your golden geese, but it's well worth it down the road.

Step #5: Monitor your money management plan.
The final step involves monitoring your money management by keeping track of both your cash flow and your net worth.

Your cash flow analysis

An important aspect of controlling your money and being successful in the world of finances is keeping tabs on your cash flow on a regular basis. Your cash flow analysis is a written plan of how you spend your money. It's a simple cost-breakdown of your expenses, as seen in most budgets, and involves tracking your income and expenses on a monthly basis.

Unlike a simple budget, your cash flow analysis allows you to see the effects of how you allocate your monetary resources to your bottom line several months down the road. This analysis now becomes a great predictive tool as to how you can better budget your money.

Your cash flow analysis should take into account several important factors, such as:
- Your budget priorities as a family, based on your passions and dreams.
- The impact of your specific family values on your cash flow. and
- The specific short-term budgeting plans, as well as long-term projections over a six-month to one-year period.

The easiest way to keep track of your cash flow is to use a simple electronic spreadsheet. The most significant advantage in using an electronic spreadsheet is that you are able to see the effects of purchasing decisions being made today on your cash flow five or six months out.

Stanley and **Danko** in the **Millionaire Next Door** talk about the importance that many self-made millionaires have placed on keeping tabs on their financial affairs on a regular basis. Here are some of the specific benefits of tracking your finances on a spreadsheet for you to consider:

- Gain peace of mind knowing how easy it is to monitor one's cash flow.
- Build greater confidence in managing your affairs more effectively.
- Readily see the long-term effects of changing either one's expenses or revenue.
- Quickly identify expenses that need to be monitored more closely.

Your first step in using an electronic spreadsheet is to pull out any information about your currently established monthly withdrawals, such as your rent or mortgage payments, insurance, car payments, etc. Try to compile a list of your actual, monthly expenses, as well as your current sources of revenue.

Keep in mind that this is a predictive tool, not a cast-in-stone budget to follow religiously. Once you have at least two months of actual data in your file you'll be in a better position to extend your projections out to four to six months. Play around with the spreadsheet that you'll create to give you more predictive power as to how your finances could unfold, based on your monetary decisions.

Tracking your net worth
Besides monitoring your cash flow, it is important to periodically assess your net worth.

The measure of true wealth is not in how many material possessions you have acquired. True wealth is a function of the relationship between your assets, or money flowing into your "piggy bank," versus liabilities, where money is being emptied from your "piggy bank."

To calculate your net worth, you need to total up the assets you possess and subtract your liabilities. Assets typically show up in categories such as investments, bank accounts, pension plans, chattels or equity in your personal residence. On the other hand, liabilities include such categories as credit card debt, long-term loans, home mortgage, taxes owing or unpaid bills.

I suggest that you calculate your net worth right now and then monitor your net worth every three to four months. Most financial institutions and financial planners will be able to help you keep track of your net worth, either by charting your assets and liabilities on paper or by entering this information into an electronic spreadsheet.

Keep in mind that what you focus your attention on will increase. If you monitor your cash flow and net worth you'll see positive change occurring within a very short period of time. Now let's take a look at the relationship between your current state of affairs and where you would like to be.

Your Gap Analysis:
Several years ago, I came across **Loral Langemeier's** book **The Millionaire Maker** in which she outlines how to determine the gap between where you are at in your wealth creation process and where you want to be. In other words, what is your current financial baseline and what do you need your investments to produce income-wise in order to reach a point of financial freedom or generate a certain amount of cash flow to meet your needs.

By assessing your monthly cash flow projections as well as determining your current net worth, you now have a framework upon which to determine the gap that exists between your current financial situation and where you would like to be.

Try using this simple mental framework from which to organize all of this information.

Create Your REAL Financial Picture:
To get a clear picture of your REAL financial situation start by looking at your sources of **R**evenue, your current monthly **E**xpenditures, and your net worth which is made up of your **A**ssets and **L**iabilities.

Once you have an idea as to your starting point, your next step is to determine how much income you require from your investments in order to support your desired lifestyle. In essence, you're determining the point in your financial affairs whereby you reach critical mass with your cash-flowing investments. This could be cash coming from stocks, real estate, hard assets or systematized businesses.

I recommend starting with a calculation that is based on an average expected return of 15% from your cash flowing investments that is ear-marked to support your lifestyle.

Therefore, you need to determine a minimum investment base that allows you to consistently generate this level of return. This investment base is your point at which you just reach critical mass with the invested capital on hand, working for you to create your desired lifestyle.

As you learn and implement the concepts presented in this book, you may find that achieving an average annual return of 15% is lower than what you're capable of consistently achieving in the stock market. This allows you to not only pay for your desired lifestyle, but also to account for the effects of inflation, as well as grow your wealth at the same time.

For example, if you deem that you would require $45,000 from your investment holdings excluding any company or government pensions, this equates to a capital base of $300,000. Once you have amassed this level of capital, you have reached the lower threshold of your critical mass point.

This point is a far cry from what the financial services industry would like you to believe that you need in order to retire comfortably. Many in the industry advocate amassing a million-dollar fortune before being able to retire comfortably.

It never ceases to amaze me that just a few skills and a little financial education can make the difference from being able to enjoy your life to the fullest vs. a life based on the popular 40-40-40 formula. The 40-40-40 formula is based on the notion that after working 40 hours per week for 40 years, you get to retire on 40% of what you may have set aside in mutual funds, bonds and your bank account. Not a very inviting formula at that, isn't it?

An accelerated cash flow system that taps into the benefits of investing in individual stocks and layering on cash-flowing option positions provides a much better future outlook. Now let's explore how you can ramp up your investment process.

Saving to Invest:
Are you currently cash poor, yet investment opportunity rich? The challenge that faces many investors is the inability to take advantage of stock investment opportunities as they present themselves. You may find yourself currently in this situation.

Very few American families place saving as the #1 financial priority for the household. But the truth of the matter is that if you do not have any savings set aside, you cannot invest. If you cannot invest, you dash any hopes of becoming financially free and building the lifestyle you've always dreamt about.

Start today by looking at saving as being a positive active process and not a passive activity. Why? It requires effort to properly manage your money. Saving to invest opens up new possibilities. Those possibilities allow you to look forward to working towards realizing your dreams.

So, how could you ramp up your savings and better position your capital to take advantage of investment opportunities? Here are 4 approaches to consider, in order of priority:

Approach #1: Automatic Contribution:
Get into the mindset of always paying yourself first. Make your saving process as automatic and disciplined as possible.
1. Automatic - by regularly transferring your earned income into a dedicated savings account earmarked for investing.
2. Disciplined - by using that money to only invest in 3 types of opportunities that will move you forward, namely:
- Your investments, such as stocks and options.
- Your financial education through books, programs, seminars or coaching.
- Your own cash flowing business.

As well, learn to live below your means but within your needs. By having a frugal approach to spending you create a more positive saving routine for yourself.

Approach #2: Sell Stuff around the Home.
Consider selling something of value in order to raise some cash in the short-term for investment purposes. Do you have recreational vehicles, an extra TV or spare furniture that you could sell on Craigslist, Kijiji or some other platform?

Realize that this is a short-term sacrifice that empowers you to start building wealth. Keep in mind that you can always treat yourself later once your financial affairs are in order and you have learned how to consistently grow your money through investing.

Approach #3: Make More Money.

Increase your income over time by:

- Adding more value in the workplace and then asking for a pay increase.
- Or getting a part-time job specifically for reducing your bad debt and for your investing.

It's important to allocate the majority of your additional cash for investment purposes. Sure, go ahead and reward your hard efforts by spending a small portion of your additional income on creating lasting memories, However, do not fail to lose sight of your initial goal. Stay true to your saving to invest discipline. Your long-term sustainable wealth could very well depend on it.

Approach #4: Leverage OPM.

Honestly, this is my least favorite approach of the four being mentioned. As a last resort, consider using OPM - Other People's Money (not the drug) - to help build your investment portfolio. They say that a lifelong friend is someone you haven't borrowed money from yet. Friends and family can be another plausible source of funds to tap into. Especially if you have a large, loving, caring, close-knit family in another city.

If you're looking at getting a personal loan or line of credit for strictly investment purposes, do so only if you can comfortably meet the following four criteria:

1. If the loan interest rate is no more than 1/3 your expected rate of return on your investment. For example, if you anticipate generating a 15% overall return selling covered

call options, you should not take on a loan that exceeds 5 or 6%.

2. If your loan can be easily paid off within 1 year from your annual savings.
3. If you have your bad debt under control from your credit cards and consumer loans.
4. If you have a proven track record of managing your money well - you need to be honest with yourself on this one. Right?

True, banks are a source of funds. However, most banks will lend you money only if you can prove you don't need it. This may be a tough course of action to pursue.

Another source of funds to possibly consider is peer-to-peer lending clubs that are popping up online. Although I have no personal experience with this form of acquiring investment capital, I mention it as a possibility. One caveat though. Do your due diligence on the organization before getting involved.

And what does that mean? Check out the section of your book that addresses how to avoid being scammed. I have a personal stake in spreading the word about how not to get ripped off.

Hopefully, at least one of these four approaches will resonate with you and inspire you to take the next step, that of actively saving for investment purposes.

Debt Reduction "is" a Priority:
What is the worst barrier to successful investing? Simply put, the effects of bad debt.

By eliminating bad debt more of your hard-earned dollars can be set aside for investments. The sooner you begin this process the more effective you'll become in compounding your investment returns over the years.

From a money management perspective, there is both good and bad debt. Good debt is money you borrow at a low interest rate and then invest it at a higher rate of return. You are using other people's money as leverage to make you money.

Bad debt or consumer debt is money you borrow at a high interest rate to buy things that don't produce income or grow in value. It's the effect of compounding rates of return working against you instead of for you that becomes a financial drain.

For example, if you are paying 18 percent for your credit card debt and trying to make 15 percent on your stock investments, you end up going backwards at a rate of 3 percent compounded per year.

The sooner that you take the necessary steps to eliminate your bad debt out of the investment equation the faster you can move towards reaching a point of financial freedom. Another tool that I found to be effective from **Loral Langemeier's** book **The Millionaire Maker** was her debt reduction plan that I'll share with you right now.

Five-Step Debt Elimination Strategy:
According to **Loral** some of the worst strategies for eliminating debt are:

- Transferring debt from a high-interest-rate credit card to a lower interest-rate credit card. With this strategy the root of the problem, systematically paying off the debt obligation, is not being dealt with.
- Refinancing the home to consolidate debt. This approach still does not address the problem of controlling one's spending.

- Allowing a debt-consolidation company to create one very comfortable monthly payment. Unfortunately, with the low payments the principal never gets paid down in a reasonable period of time.
- Declaring bankruptcy. This can seriously disrupt your life, ruin your credit and   severely impair your ability to build wealth.

So, what is your best choice given the myriad of debt reduction tips and advice out in the market today? *Loral* describes an effective five-step debt elimination strategy.

What I like about her strategy is that it's easy to implement and actually works, speaking from personal experience. After retiring from the work force and then being scammed shortly thereafter of my life savings back in 2007, I needed an effective system to completely eliminate the massive credit card debt that had built up. *Loral's* strategy allowed me to pay down all of my consumer debt within the next year. Thanks *Loral*.

Step #1: Document Your Debt Obligations.
Set up a table or spreadsheet and list all of your consumer debt, including credit cards, charge accounts, loans that are not held against an asset and any other outstanding liabilities. Fill in the table with the name of the creditor, the current amount owing, the minimum monthly payment and the interest rate being charged.

In the following example, I'll use Visa and MasterCard credit card debts to show you how the system works.

Step #2: Calculate Your Factoring Number.
For each debt obligation divide the amount of debt owed by your monthly minimum payment. For example, if you owe $5000 on your Visa credit card that has a monthly minimum payment of

$250, your factoring number would be 5000 divided by 250 which is 20. This number roughly represents the number of months that it would take in order to pay off the debt by paying only the minimum payment required. Should your MasterCard have an outstanding balance of $1500 and monthly minimum payment of $100, your MasterCard factoring number would be 15 (which is less than that for Visa).

Step #3: Prioritize Your Debt.
Place the debt that has the highest factor at the top of your list, in this case the Visa card. The debt with the second lowest factor would be placed just below. The third lowest factor would occupy the third rang and so on.

Step #4: Jump Start Your Allocations.
In addition to the minimum payments required, you're going to take $200 from your current spending and apply that to eliminating your bad debt. The $200 additional contribution is a reasonable level to achieve, which can be accomplished by either cutting back expenses, selling a few household items or through part-time work as previously outlined in the chapter.

Step #5: Debt Payments.
Pay off the minimum payment for each debt obligation each month. In addition to the minimum payments for your highest ranked debt, use the $200 additional contribution to pay this off.

For example, if you your highest ranked debt according to your factor number requires that you pay a minimum of $250 that month do so, but also apply the additional $200 to this payment making it a total of $450 for that month. In our example, you would pay off your Visa card minimum balance plus an additional $200.

Continue to pay off the top-ranked debt until fully eliminated. Once your highest debt obligation is paid off you apply this amount, which in our example was $450 to the second highest debt obligation. For example, if your MasterCard requires a minimum payment of $100 you would pay this plus the $450 for a total of $550.

As you can see the payments build as each debt obligation is paid off. This process accelerates your debt reduction while maintaining the same level of financing set aside each month for debt.

The key to this plan is to commit to making your monthly payments plus the specific jump start allocation. As you pay off each debt completely, the money initially set aside for that particular debt obligation is allocated to accelerate the pay down of the next highest debt. This accelerated debt elimination system works well within the framework of the accelerated cash flow system you'll be introduced to in the next chapter. Both systems increase the velocity of your money to achieve specific financial outcomes faster.

Making the Best of Your 401(k) & IRA:

Two of the most common investment accounts for retirement are the 401(K) and the IRA. Knowing which account to use in various investment situations can be tricky. Here are some simple investment account tips that might point you in the right direction to maximize your returns and minimize your future tax burden.

There are several main advantages in contributing to a 401(K).
- You can deposit a lot of money each year compared to other plans.
- Your employer can match funds that you deposit up to a set maximum.

- Nobody can touch the money, even if you go bankrupt.
- Most employers allow you to borrow your own money, paying back the loan over time.
- Contributions come from pre-tax income, so you don't get taxed on the money going in.

The downside is that:
- Most plans are very limited in the investment choices that you have. You're typically limited to a few mutual funds and bonds.
- The average 401(K) fees are 1.5 percent off the top every year. This small amount ends up reducing your potential gains by 40 - 60 percent over time. Yes, you heard me right, your potential returns will be eroded by 40 to 60 percent depending on the time frame selected. This is one major reason why you can do better on your own with a self-directed investment account.

So how do we maximize our profitability in our 401(K) accounts?

If your employer is matching your contributions, then you should contribute money to your plan up to the set maximum for matching funds.

If your company offers a Roth 401(k), then your best bet may be to opt in for this plan as it allows you make withdrawals after age 59 ½ tax free, as opposed to being tax deferred. Having tax-free income in retirement is a great option to have whether or not tax rates will change in the future. My personal feeling is that tax rates will probably increase in the future as opposed to decrease. Of course, the main disadvantage is that the contributions come out of your paycheck after taxes have been removed.

In either 401(k) plans, choose either a low-cost Index Fund that mirrors a broad index like the S&P 500 or possibly get some bond exposure by buying specific bonds. Avoid actively managed mutual funds, since the management fees will erode your profit potential substantially over time.

Avoid both target-date retirement funds and bond funds. Target-date funds create a blend of stock and bond funds based on your retirement date, with a higher allocation to bond funds as you approach retirement. The problem is that long-term bond funds have no set maturity date; therefore, you have less of a guarantee that you'll get your principal back as with individual bonds. This is just one risk factor that you need to be aware of when working with funds.

After you have maxed out your 401(K) matching contributions, the next strategy is to make contributions to an Individual Retirement Account (IRA). An IRA provides you with several key advantages, namely:

- You have greater flexibility as to what investments you can hold within your account, especially with individual stocks.
- It allows almost anyone who has earned income to invest.
- The contributions to a Traditional IRA come from pre-tax income, so under most conditions you don't get taxed on the money going in.
- Most IRA accounts allow you to sell covered calls, which provides you with a powerful investment platform from which to implement the accelerated cash flow system.

Given the choice of different types of IRA accounts, consider opening up a Roth IRA instead of a traditional one. The two major advantages of using a Roth IRA are that:

- The earnings are tax-free instead of tax-deferred. As already mentioned, this can be significant 10, 20 or even 30 years down the road.

- You can take out your original contributions any time you want, regardless of your age, without taxes and penalties.

In a nutshell, we're all born free and then you're taxed to death. So, it makes sense to structure your investment portfolios to reduce the effects of taxation on your holdings.

You'll need to set up an account with an online discount broker if you haven't done so already. Start by doing a little comparative research online. This should yield a couple of promising discount brokers who offer low stock and option transaction fees. Select a solid broker who does offer low fees. Higher fees can erode your cash flow potential over time. As the martial arts master says to his young accolade: "Choose wisely Grasshopper."

It's in your IRA account that you'll benefit the most from building a portfolio of stocks, especially if the capital appreciation is able to grow tax-free until you need it in retirement. All discount brokers will allow you to sell calls from within your IRA, which is a key component of the accelerated cash flow system. Please contact your specific online broker to find out what you can and cannot do within your IRA account. Guidelines change from time to time. There you have it in a nutshell, a few simple strategies to incorporate into your overall investment plan.

Are You Canadian, eh?

Making the Best of Your RRSP & TFSA:
The most common Canadian investment account for retirement is the Registered Retirement Savings Plan or RRSP. However, another savings program that has gained in popularity is the Tax-Free Savings Account. Here are some simple investment account tips that'll give you greater insight into how to use each type of account. There are several main advantages in contributing to a RRSP:

- You can contribute a high percentage of earned income each year based on the lower of 18% of earned income or a fixed cap, which has been indexed to be slightly over $26,000.
- You receive a tax credit that reduces your taxable income by the amount you contribute.
- You are able to defer paying any tax until funds are withdrawn, which is normally at retirement thus allowing your returns to compound tax free over time.
- You can borrow funds from your account to purchase a home or pay for post-secondary education.
- You have the flexibility of holding many different types of investments within the account.
- You can swap investments between another investment portfolio and your RRSP account.
- You don't lose your contribution room. Any unused contributions are carried forward to your future deduction limits until age 71.

The downside of an RRSP is that:
- There is a lack of liquidity should you need to use your funds. The tax consequences for early withdrawals can be serious with withholding taxes in the range of 10 to 30%, in addition to your income tax payable.
- You can't take advantage of the dividend tax credit on eligible shares that are part of an RRSP. As well, the full amount of capital gains realized within a RRSP is eventually fully taxable at retirement or withdrawal. Capital gains that are not part of an RRSP are subject to income tax on only 50% of the gain, excluding your tax-free savings account. The bottom line? This means that any growth in your RRSP will be eventually taxed at the highest level, that of earned income.

So how do we maximize your profitability potential in your RRSP account?

Your first order of business is to select the right RRSP account. You have two basic choices: a "managed" account, which is usually offered by major financial institutions and mutual fund companies or a "self-directed" account, typically offered by discount brokers.

A managed account limits your investment options to primarily two types of investments, namely mutual fund products and fixed-income investments such as guaranteed investment certificates or GICs.

By choosing a self-directed RRSP you open up your investment possibilities to being able to use the cash flow strategies outlined in this program. For example, from within a self-directed RRSP you'll be able to invest in individual stocks and covered call contracts. Your best bet is to set up your self-directed account with a discount broker thus allowing you access to not only a myriad of investment choices but also low transaction fees that will help to keep your costs down.

Optimizing Your Tax-Free Savings Account:
Most investors are unaware of the growth potential that a simple tax-free savings account can offer a savvy investor. Many use the account as a simple savings program rather than using it to their full advantage. Properly structured, a TFSA can be used to hold quality dividend-paying stocks, or any market leading stock for that matter, and even allow you to sell covered calls. We'll get into options strategies more in the next chapter.

Suffice it to say that the beauty of the TFSA is that any growth is tax exempt, which means that you can use the power of compounding from within the account to accelerate your wealth building even faster.

The account is very liquid, allowing you the flexibility to make withdrawals without penalty. The one limiting factor is that you'll need to wait until January of the following year in order to make any additional contributions up to your allowable limit. The best part is that when you withdraw your funds you won't have to pay any income tax on the withdrawal.

The two biggest limitations of the TFSA are that:
- The maximum annual contribution limit is currently $5500 (2018) per person.
- Any contributions made are done so with money that has already been taxed.

So how can we take advantage of the benefits of these various types of accounts? I believe that every Canadian should try to capitalize on the advantages offered by each account.

The TFSA allows you to slowly build a portfolio of stock holdings over time since you're only allowed to contribute $5,500 per year. The biggest advantage is that any gains made in your account are tax free. That will be a huge advantage down the road as you approach retirement.

Your self-directed RRSP also offers great flexibility in terms of being able to use the various cash flow strategies outlined in this program. It allows you to buy quality dividend-paying stocks and then sell monthly covered calls in order to generate a cash flow stream from both the quarterly dividend payments and the monthly option premiums. This account makes sense for someone wanting to compound their gains over time.

The third type of account that unfortunately receives no preferential tax treatment is an option account set up with your discount broker. This account gives you the greatest flexibility of investment strategies to employ. You'll also be able to take advantage of the 50% exclusion rule on capital gains and the dividend tax credit on eligible dividends. Eligible dividends are those paid by Canadian companies to Canadian tax payers; therefore, foreign companies such as Intel or McDonalds are unfortunately exempt.

At a bare minimum, an accelerated cash flow investor should open up a self-directed RRSP and TFSA that allows stock and option plays. To get a better feel for what each account has to offer and what the rules, regulations and tax implications are for each account, go to the Revenue Canada website.

Let's now take a look at how you can enlist the help of others in order to move you closer to achieving your core desires and realizing your dreams.

Seven Selective Steps to Choosing the Right Financial Advisor:
Having a strong supportive team of professionals that you can turn to for sound advice moves you closer to being successful in whatever future endeavors you may pursue. A financial advisor is one such key player who can help guide you through many investment or financial decisions. In identifying someone who is able to work with you (an active investor) requires a little preparation.

DeMarco stresses that a financial advisor does not fix financial illiteracy. He says: Literacy gives you the power to evaluate your advisor's advice."

Unfortunately, most financial advisors prefer selling you their line of products based on a fee or commission structure. This might be great if you're a passive investor willing to turn your money over to a professional to manage. However, this is not what I recommend that you do. Once you learn how to manage your money and investments on your own, you won't want to settle for market returns when you can do substantially better with just a little more effort.

Should you consider using the services of a professional, you may be best served in areas where their expertise fills a void in your current knowledge base. This could be in the realm of financial planning, insurance needs, structuring investment accounts or tax advice. With so many individuals hanging up their "Investment Advisor" or "Financial Planner" shingles on their walls, how do you wade through those self-serving salesmen to find someone who has your best interests at heart?

Here are seven selective steps to finding the right financial advisor to meet your needs:

Step #1: Get Recommendations.
Start by compiling a list of potential candidates that you can contact as part of your initial screening process. Ask your close friends, colleagues and family members to suggest potential candidates. At this stage of the game, get some basic contact and background information on each possible advisor.

Step #2: Screen Your Recommendations.
From your list of good contacts try to touch base by phone to get a preliminary "read" on the individual. If you find that you have made a connection over the phone with someone who may be able to help, then schedule a face-to-face meeting.

Step #3: Meet and Greet.

Arrange to meet your potential candidate in his or her office. This enables you to assess the "outward" appearance of the office, the staff and your advisor in a professional setting. Ideally, you are looking for someone who is a strong role model. For example, is the financial advisor dressed for success? Also, watch and observe how people in the office interact and carry themselves. You can learn a lot about the prospective candidate even before setting foot in his or her office for the meeting.

Step #4: Ask a Lot of Questions.

Before arriving in the office take some time to craft a list of questions that'll enable you to better acquaint yourself with the advisor. You should try to assess the depth of knowledge, wealth of experience and underlying investment philosophy that drives the advisor. Try to assess if there will be a good personality fit between the two of you. This is critical to establishing a profitable life-long relationship for both parties.

Take the time to assess the advisor's familiarity with and ability to discuss and recommend a wide variety of investment products, such as bonds, stocks, options and commodities. Is your advisor trying to steer you only toward mutual funds? Above all, don't forget whose money and financial well-being it is, and who should profit from it.

Step #5: Follow K.I.S.S. - Keeping Investment Statements Simple Principle.

Ask to see a sample copy of the firm's or advisor's client statements. Is it easy to understand? Does the statement clearly show you what assets you own, the value and the gains/losses made? What other tools does the advisor provide to help you track your investments or financial products?

Step #6: Compensation?

Find out how your advisor will be compensated for various types of transactions and services performed. If by commissions, are those commissions negotiable under some circumstances?

Step #7: Get Testimonials.

Ask your advisor if he or she could provide you with some testimonials, such as a recent letter of gratitude or recommendation. Being able to get a third-party endorsement moves you closer to making the right decision.

Taking the time to find the right individual who is willing to work with you as a member of your overall investment team is well worth the time spent. The right individual should be able to steer you in the right direction and hold you accountable for achieving your investment goals.

As you gain more investment knowledge and experience, you may wish to seek out more members to your investment team who will help you evolve and reach your full potential as an investor. Just as a financial advisor may come in handy in rounding out those areas where you require some additional expertise, so too do mentors or like-minded friends provide a similar service. Keep an eye out for those individuals who can move you to the next level of your personal development as a successful investor.

Eight Tips on How to Avoid Being Scammed:

This topic resonates deeply with me on a personal level since back in 2007, I lost my entire self-directed retirement portfolio to a group of financial predators. Even though I believed that I had done enough due diligence on the organization by checking government websites, talking to other investors, visiting the corporate office, and attending conferences, I was still swindled out of my life savings. Ouch!

I feel that it's important for me to share what I've learned from this personal tragedy, so that you do not succumb to the sales pitches of the shady, slick promoters out in the world of investing. By knowing how to do your due diligence on any investment opportunity you'll be in a better position to invest in those safe investment vehicles that'll move you closer to being financially secure.

As an investor, there is nothing worse than the feeling you get in the pit of your stomach knowing that you have been scammed out of your life savings. While assessing what went wrong, one experiences a flood of emotions - disbelief, disgust, anger and despair.

How does one even consider bouncing back from such a set-back? More importantly, how should you protect yourself from future scams? We've all heard the rhyme, "Fool me once, shame on you. Fool me twice, shame on me."

Fundamental to the process of investing in any opportunity is the notion of doing your due diligence. You must personally undertake the necessary research to assess the viability of any opportunity before committing capital whether it be in the stock market, real estate, commodities or businesses.

The following 8 tips should help you avoid any shocking surprises: *Tip #1:* Determine the extent to which you have control over access to your capital. Are there any suspicious procedures or conditions in place? For example, are you being told that you can easily tap into your 401K (or RRSP) to finance this "once in a lifetime" opportunity? Never fall for an investment scheme to extract money out of your 401K (or RRSP). You'll probably get an unexpected tax bill from the IRS (or CRA).

Tip #2: Check with the local securities commission as to the legitimacy of the promoters and the opportunity. Verify the track record of the business entity by looking into the historical record of SEC filings. Does anything unusual pop up as far as excessive liabilities, negative cash flow, declining growth rates over time? Have any complaints been lodged in the past? You'll also be able to assess whether or not the investment is compliant with federal laws by contacting the SEC.

Tip #3: Is the promoter sporting the latest Armani suit and Rolex watch? Do not be overly impressed with first impressions. Many of these slick salesmen have acquired their wealth off of the backs of others and not necessarily through investing prowess. You can also Google the names of the promoters and the business for any negative press out on the internet.

Tip #4: How simple is the investment? Be wary of complicated structures that are out of the ordinary. Are you confused about how the opportunity will generate the promised high returns? Never invest in something you do not understand. There are a finite number of ways to legally make money through investing. You should be able to match the proposed strategy to a well-established time-tested one that can be explained in simple terms.

Tip #5: Are you required to move money off-shore, set up an elaborate money management system or provide your personal banking information? As a word of caution, do not send money over the internet without doing extensive due diligence. If you're being told that the money is going to a "tax haven status" country so that your assets are protected from the clutches of the taxman, don't believe it. International banking is becoming more and more transparent with countries sharing increasing amounts of information about their respective citizens.

Tip #6: Do you have to make a decision right away or lose out on getting in on the opportunity all together? If you're being pressured to act now - don't - run the other way instead. No worthwhile opportunity should require a split-second snap decision. Don't succumb to time pressures to sign any papers without having the opportunity to methodically comb through the paperwork looking for reasons why this opportunity may not be in your best interests. Always insist on doing your own due diligence on any investment opportunity.

Tip #7: Are you being promised an incredible rate of return on your invested capital with little or no downside risk? If it sounds too good to be true, it probably is. Ask yourself: Does this particular opportunity fit in with what you would normally expect to receive as a return on your investment from similar products or offers? Especially be cautious of verbal guarantees of amazing returns with no documented proof that can be verified independently. As well, compare what has been verbally promised to what is in writing. Talk is cheap. Read any and all documents thoroughly before signing.

Tip #8: Is someone from the same organization or affinity group that you belong to heavily promoting the opportunity based on your affiliation? Beware of investments sold through service clubs, religious groups and community organizations. We tend to let our guard down when we are a part of an organization built on trust and mutual respect. Self-serving slick promoters are quick to capitalize on this weakness.

To wrap up, following these 8 tips will help keep those financial wolves at bay. I trust that you'll be able to share these invaluable lessons with your family members in the hopes of protecting your and their hard-earned money. Wouldn't you agree?

Four Phases of Wealth Creation:

A couple of common questions that I often receive are: Why even bother trying to figure out how to invest? Won't my employer and the government provide for me upon retirement?

The harsh reality is that the government has made it perfectly clear that the shift in responsibility for your economic well-being is upon your shoulders. Even though social security will probably be in place decades down the road, your ability to tap into it may be postponed until you are well into your 70's, especially if you are currently in your 20's or 30's.

So how should we look at a lifetime of investing if we're to create enough wealth to enjoy life to the fullest? Here's some sage advice pertaining to each of the four phases of wealth creation:

Phase #1: Contribution.

This phase is characterized by two major aspects of wealth creation, namely:

- The learning years where you focus on acquiring the necessary education that enables you to generate wealth.
- The earning years where you begin to save a portion of your income for investment purposes.

These two aspects typically begin in your early 20's. Some positive habits to develop from the get go are to:

1. Pay yourself first by targeting a portion of your earnings for investments as soon as the money is made available. In other words, investing becomes a priority money management item.
2. Save and earmark at least 10% of your earnings for future investments.

3. Invest in opportunities that either further your investment education or consistently grow your capital, such as through the stock market or rental real estate.

During these learning years, you should begin by investing in the wealth creation sector that:
- You're the most passionate about learning more.
- You have the most initial knowledge and experience.
- Is the most applicable to tap into your current skills, abilities and talents.

In doing so, you increase the likelihood that you'll become a more dedicated and successful investor. Once you finish reading this book, you'll be in a better position to determine if stock investing for cash flow resonates with you.

Phase #2: Accumulation.

This phase usually occupies a major portion of your life. It is characterized by the systematic investment of your actively earned income into investment vehicles that:
- Generate passive income through dividends and/ or option premiums in the stock market, through rental real estate or through a systematized business that requires little hands on activity.
- Grow your initial capital through asset appreciation.
- Compound both the interest earned and capital appreciation over time.

Look for opportunities that will either provide a:
- Tax deduction on the initial investment.
- Tax deferral of the interest or appreciation generated until a future date.
- Tax exemption on the interest or appreciation generated.

This can be accomplished through vehicles such as a 401(k), Roth IRA, RRSP (Canada), TFSA (Canada) universal life insurance policy and your principal residence.

Phase #3: Distribution.

As you approach retirement, your focus shifts from saving and investing to the preservation of your assets and the protection of your "true wealth". True wealth can be expressed as your ability to:

- Create a set of values to live by that reflect your integrity as a member of our society.
- Create value for those lives you touch over the course of your lifetime.
- Assess value in being able to take advantage of opportunities that move you closer to being financially free.
- Benefit from the value that you have created in sharing the moments, time and memories with loved ones.

During the distribution phase, you should structure the systematic withdrawal of your retirement capital such that it will have little or no impact on your nest egg. This can be accomplished through properly structured universal life insurance policies, family trusts, tax-exempt investment accounts and incorporated business structures.

Phase #4: Transfer.

Yes! Death is hereditary. As they say: "Where there's a will, there are 500 relatives." If you've planned your retirement properly, as you approach the end of your earthly existence, you'll be in the enviable position to pass on your wealth to loved ones and/or your favorite charities. To better preserve your legacy, ensure that you empower your family members with the stewardship and accountability for perpetuating the wealth that you have generated. In doing so, you'll have lived life to the fullest.

There you have it, a quick snapshot of the four major wealth creation phases. Whether you're just starting out or moving closer to retirement, this chapter has provided you with a number of money management strategies and tools that'll serve you well down the road.

When you begin to take back control of your financial affairs so that your debt level is now manageable and you're amassing capital ear-marked for investing, you position yourself to reach your full potential as an investor.

The next chapter delves into learning new wealth generation skills that focus on accelerating your money through better and better investment opportunities presented by the stock market.

Chapter 4 - Becoming Acquainted with the FAST Approach

Focus Questions:
1. What are the different ways of investing in the stock market?
2. What two investment approaches will accelerate your wealth the fastest?
3. Why should dividend stocks be at the core of your wealth creation?
4. What are covered calls and why should you sell them?

Before we get into the details of the FAST approach, let's back up and give you a quick overview of the three most common investment approaches. A simplistic view of how you can invest in the stock market is to look at three current practices used extensively by most investors. These three approaches are value, income and growth investing.

Each approach provides the investor with different investment opportunities offering:
- Different risk - reward profiles.
- Varying investment holding periods.
- And the use of various stock investment strategies.

The following is a simplified explanation of these common approaches.

Value Investing:
The primary objective of value investing is to acquire undervalued businesses below fair market price and hold them long-term until they can be sold above their true intrinsic value at a profit.

The key factors of value investing are that:

1. The primary focus is on capital preservation by buying the business with a large margin of safety below its fair market price. A margin of safety refers to a current stock price that is typically 30% or more less than the stock's estimated intrinsic value or retail price.
2. Select businesses with solid fundamentals in the areas of book value, debt levels, and return on capital invested over a minimum 5-year period.
3. The holding period is long-term, typically 5 - 10 years.
4. The type of investor favored is one with a low risk tolerance and who is patient and disciplined.
5. You profit best from the stock price cycling from being undervalued to overvalued.

Income Investing:
The objective of income investing is to create a regular, income stream from typically mature companies who consistently pay a portion of profits back to the shareholders in the form of dividends. The key factors of income investing are that:
1. The primary focus is on regular income production, at least quarterly, with an emphasis on capital preservation by investing in companies that have a long solid track record.
2. Select mature businesses with consistent earnings, sales and cash flow over long periods of 10 to 20 years that have a historical record of paying good dividends.
3. The holding period is usually long-term, typically greater than 10 years.
4. The type of investor favored is one with a low risk tolerance, who is typically looking for income generation, such as in retirement or helping to fund a college education.
5. You profit best from mature businesses that are not greatly affected by economic cycles and who have a solid track record of consistently paying out dividends.

Growth Investing:

The primary objective of growth investing is to acquire businesses experiencing higher than market average earnings growth due to a major change affecting the industry. Ideally, the investor would like to select businesses in their infancy of their growth phase. They have the greatest potential to grow and become more stable mature companies down the road.

The key factors of growth investing are that:

1. The primary focus is on capital appreciation through increased share price in companies experiencing a major positive change in their industry. This typically happens as a result of new technological breakthroughs, new market trends or expanding international markets.
2. Select specialized businesses or industries experiencing positive change and that have superior growth in earnings, sales and a strong possibility of high growth of invested capital.
3. The holding period is often medium-term, typically 2 - 5 years.
4. The type of investor favored is one with a moderate risk tolerance who is typically looking for capital appreciation.
5. You profit best from younger companies that are seeing the benefits from a major market change that is enabling them to grow earnings and invested capital above the market average.

All three approaches have their place in an investor's portfolio, whether you're just starting out or you're at the end of your pursuit as an active investor. Having said that, the question that begs to be answered is so how does an accelerated cash flow system differ from the above general investment approaches?

How does an Accelerated Cash Flow System fit in?
In a nutshell, an accelerated cash flow system is based on an income and growth approach that incorporates option strategies to generate higher returns than any one approach on its own.

The basic premise behind being able to accelerate your returns is that you'll build a portfolio of core growth positions. Ideally, we're looking for growing companies that are market leaders and best of breed in their respective market sector or industry.

A market leader has the general market and price momentum behind it. Many big institutional buyers look for stocks within a specific sector or industry that the overall market has fallen in love with. These stocks are in favour as evidenced by a positive growing trend in world demand for the products or services being offered.

For example, in 2011 and 2012 the mobile internet was one growing trend worldwide that had many technology stocks moving higher as a result of being in favour with the overall market players.

The companies that are market leaders are those that are benefiting the most from the sale of their products and services in the worldwide market. They also tend to be the best of breed businesses within their industry. A best of breed business is one that has:
1. Solid fundamentals.
This shows up in the key ratios that are showing consistent double-digit growth rates and long-term debt levels that are under control.

2. A solid management team.

Here we're looking for a CEO who comes across as having his/her shareholder's interest at heart and not his/her ego or the bonuses he/she might receive.

3. A competitive advantage.

Having a sustainable competitive advantage sets any business apart from other companies that are just along for the ride in a trending market. Determining if a company has a significant competitive advantage is easily verified by looking at the growth rates for earnings, sales, cash flow and book value. More on that in a moment, okay?

Best of breed businesses have the staying power to be profitable over time, which in turn increases your profitability potential as an investor. We'll take a look at how to spot these businesses in the next chapter. An accelerated cash flow approach focuses on using the momentum of the stock market to build wealth. As previously mentioned, it is based on two wealth building factors.

The first is increasing the velocity of your money by accelerating your cash flow coming from your stock holdings. This is not a buy, hold and pray strategy. Your investment dollars will move from one great business to even better ones over the course of the year. By having your investment capital generating monthly cash flow that can be re-invested into additional opportunities should you choose, you're able to create a constant stream of income flowing into your brokerage account.

As **Jim Cramer** puts it in his book **Getting Back to Even**: "Most peddlers of financial advice, even after the wealth-shattering crash of 2008, preach the virtues of owning stock just for the sake of owning them. They will tell you to buy and hold, an investing shibboleth that I have been trying to smash for ages. The buy-

and-hold strategy, if you can even call it one, is to pick a bunch of good-looking blue-chip companies, buy their stocks, and hang on to them till kingdom come. Selling is strictly forbidden. It's considered a sign of recklessness, of "trading," which all too many supposed experts think of as a dirty word. Same goes for the once-sacred mutual funds, with mangers who adopted the same careless buy-and-hold, one-decision philosophy."

The second factor is reaching a point of critical mass with your investments. Critical mass is achieved when the cash flow from your investments equals or exceeds your expenses for your desired lifestyle. This is a primary objective of this book. Enable you to generate enough cash flow so that you can live the life of your dreams and provide for your family without worry.

Which brings us to the FAST Approach to investing in the stock market.

The FAST Approach:
The FAST approach to building wealth through the stock market is simple to implement. However, optimizing it will take some effort on your part to learn the basic concepts. I'll be upfront and honest with you right now by saying that any worthwhile startegy that is going to get you from point A in your life to point B requires ongoing effort and initially some hard work to pick up the basic concepts.

My intention is to provide you with enough of an overview of the key concepts you'll need to utilize followed by those tried and true best practices that you can start implementing immediately to begin your wealth building journey. Sound reasonable? Without further ado, let's get started.

The FAST approach is your step-by-step process to follow for generating substantial cash flow from your stock investments. Once you have learned the basics, this simple template will save you time in quickly finding and assessing potential stocks. As well, this template will optimize your ability to make money in the stock market by knowing which specific strategies to employ and how to safely move into and out of positions.

Each letter in the word FAST represents a specific series of action steps, namely:

Step #1: Finding potential growth stocks.
You'll learn at least 10 ways to start identifying potential candidates for your investment portfolio.

Step #2: Assessing the growth potential of each opportunity.
I'll show you step-by-step how you can filter out those stocks that offer the greatest upside potential based on 10 popular indicators.

Step #3: Strategizing the best way to create consistent cash flow.
We'll explore how you can use stocks and options to create a sustainable stream of cash from your investments.

Step #4: Timing your entry & exit out of your positions.
We'll do this while preserving capital and generating consistent returns. I'll share with you several strategies that increase the probability of you coming out on top with each of your trades.

Before we take a look at how you can identify market leaders that are also top-notch businesses, let's step back and take a quick look at what your core positions should look like. Your primary focus when you're looking for potential investments has to be quality dividend-paying stocks.

Why Dividend Stocks?

Here's why. High dividend-paying stocks with solid fundamentals are one of the safest and fastest ways to generate a solid return in the stock market. Remember, we want to minimize various types of risk that could have a negative impact on your capital.

The following are eight compelling reasons why you should own solid dividend-paying stocks:

Reason #1: Cushions the Stock Price.

Yield support of the dividend, that is, the stock's annual dividend divided by its share price (or put another way - the interest rate paid to you), creates a cushion against selling pressure as the stock price trends lower.

The lower stock price causes a higher yield thereby encouraging value-oriented investors to step in and offset the selling. During a general downturn of the economy or a major stock market correction, those companies offering safe dividends find themselves better protected relative to the whole market.

Reason #2: Protects You from Short Sellers.

Short selling is the selling of a stock that the seller has borrowed from a broker in anticipation that the stock price will go lower. If the price drops, the short seller can buy back the stock at the lower price and make a profit on the difference.

A high dividend protects you from short-sellers, who are more reluctant to borrow money from a broker knowing that they are responsible for paying the dividend to the investor actually owning the stock. This scenario cuts into their potential profits.

Reason #3: Generates Income.

An obvious advantage is that the income you can receive from a decent yield can be significant. The fact that the company is willing to give you cash every quarter is an attractive feature.

This will prove to be a veritable cash cow in the hands of an experienced investor who knows how to milk the cash flow for what it is worth. We'll explore just how to do that in an upcoming chapter.

Reason #4: Benefit from Accidental High Yielders.

After a market crash or major pullback some companies offering small, safe dividends end up with high dividend yields because the stock price has dropped dramatically. You can sometimes tap into the income stream of those accidental high yielders that may provide you with more than 4 percent return.

It's likely that we'll experience more frequent market corrections in the future. This increased market volatility will become our friend, allowing us to take advantage of mispricing in the market.

Reason #5: Grows Your Money Faster.

Roughly 40% of the stock market's returns over long periods of time come from dividends. Not only do you benefit from capital appreciation of a "best-of-breed" stock over time, but you also receive a quarterly income from the dividend.

Dividend-yielding stocks make most sense in your IRA or 401(k) [RRSP or TFSA in Canada] retirement portfolios where you can re-invest your payouts and let them compound tax-free for decades.

Reason #6: Tax favored treatment.

A big advantage is that the taxes currently paid on dividend income are lower than those paid for earned income. Paying only 15% in tax for dividends held outside of a tax-sheltered account versus roughly double that in income tax adds up to big savings over time. This ability to minimize tax implications is an attractive feature of owning individual dividend-paying stocks.

Reason #7: Accelerates payback on the initial investment.

As dividends grow and are paid to you on a regular basis, your initial cost for your shares of stock is being paid back to you. Over time this cash flow coming back into your pocket will entirely pay for your initial investment.

At this point in time, your return on your investment now becomes infinite since you are no longer making money from your initial capital. You've already been paid back and are now in the enviable position of being able to use just the cash flow to build your wealth.

Reason #8: Hedges against inflation.

Those companies that increase their dividend payouts on a regular basis often do so at a rate above the current rate of inflation in order to keep their shareholders happy and invested. Dividends can offer you a stream of cash flow that keeps up with the rate of inflation. This preserves your future buying power of your initial investment capital.

For the active investor looking for a reasonable level of safety of principal with the upside potential to earn more from your investment, then exploring the world of dividend-producing stocks is worth the little effort involved. Wouldn't you agree?

Let's take a look at a potential scenario. If, for example, you have a stock with an initial yield of 5 %, (remember the yield represents a 5% interest rate that is deposited into your piggy bank), and if this stock grows its dividend by 12 % per year over a 10-year period, you'll have an effective yield of 15% by year 10. The effective yield is the current annual dividend payments sent to you divided by your original stock price.

Now should you not choose to have those dividends deposited into your piggy bank and decide to re-invest them and the stock appreciates in price by 10% per year, which is the 90-year average of the S&P 500, in year 10 your effective yield is now over 25%. That's powerful. Would that income stream be like getting an immediate raise for you?

Initially the effects of compounding do not have a dramatic effect. However, as the yield begins to increase and gain momentum, it really starts to take off to the point where its own momentum keeps it growing over time. You're moving towards having your entire initial investment being paid back to you.

I know that this is just a hypothetical example and most investors would be hard-pressed to hang onto a stock for 10 years. The point is that with just the combination of the reinvested growing dividends coupled with an appreciation in the stock price, you can create a significant double digit return for yourself. Imagine if we added a few more tricks up our sleeves. That could prove to be the next best thing since sliced bread.

This is the power of compounding and reaching a point of critical mass at work, which is precisely what we're going to tap into in this book. How to increase the compounding effect of your returns and be able to reach a point of critical mass with your investments, so that you can pursue your dreams under your terms.

Are you ready to move along? Now, let's take a look at how using call option strategies can further accelerate your cash flow generation.

Why Covered Calls?

As we saw with dividend-producing stocks, selling covered calls has some great benefits, such as:

Benefit #1: Tap into additional monthly or bi-monthly income.

As mentioned above, you can generate a nice stream of additional income from selling option contracts on stock that you already own. This strategy alone can generate double-digit returns for your portfolio over the course of a year.

Selling a covered call is a conservative option strategy. *Michael Thomsett* in his book *Options Trading for the Conservative Investor* says that: "The properly selected covered call strategy produces consistent current income. In exchange for writing covered calls, you risk losing out on an increased market value; when stock prices rise above strike price and calls are exercised, your shares are called away. However, when you compare that risk to the regular and dependable creation of current income in a conservative market risk profile, it is apparent that covered call writing will beat market averages without increasing market risks."

I know that was a mouthful. In a nutshell *Thomsett* touts the virtues of selling covered calls as a conservative income producing strategy in the stock market.

Benefit #2: Reduces risk.

Since you're paid a premium for renting out your stock, that cash now reduces your initial cost price or basis for the stock. Your breakeven point, should the stock decline in price, has been lowered by the amount of the premium deposited directly into your brokerage account.

In essence, you've built in a margin of safety for preserving your initial capital. Over time as you continue to write covered calls, which is another way of saying selling covered calls, your cost basis of the stock will drop to zero.

Now we're generating a cash flow from an initial investment whereby you've recovered all of your initial capital even with a stock that may not have appreciated in stock price. You're in the enviable position of playing with the house's money, as they say in Vegas. Wouldn't that be cool?

Benefit #3: Accelerates your wealth creation.

When you're able to generate a cash flow from multiple sources, such as options and dividends, this accelerates the velocity of your money in moving your capital into better and better investments. Being able to generate cash from various sources also allows you to have access to capital for opportunities when they present themselves. And did we mention the compounding effect earlier? Re-investing your proceeds gets you that much closer to reaching your point of critical mass with your investment portfolio.

As a novice options trader, there is no reason to start out learning complex strategies. Some of the simplest most conservative strategies can be the most lucrative.

One of my favorite conservative option trading strategies allows me to generate a monthly or bi-monthly income from my stock holdings. But before I share this simple strategy with you, we need to take a look at the concept of options trading.

What Are Options?

There are only two types of options - a call and a put - that can be either bought or sold. All option trading strategies are based on only these four factors. We'll be focusing our attention on just selling calls in this particular book.

By using a very conservative call option strategy that of selling covered calls in conjunction with your dividend-paying stock, you can create some additional monthly income to supplement your quarterly payouts. This strategy works well when the markets are slowing trending upward (what is known as a bullish trend) or the markets are going nowhere - being essentially flat month to month.

The call option strategy of selling covered calls is simple to implement. The basic idea is to "rent out" your shares of stock on a monthly or bi-monthly basis, in which you're paid a premium up front (the rent) in doing so. To rent out your shares, you must own at least 100 shares of stock for every option contract that you sell. Following me so far?

When you sell your contract, the buyer on the other end of the transaction now has the right to buy your stock at a specified fixed price, known as the strike price. The buyer can do so only when the stock price is at or above the strike price by a specific date known as the expiration date. The buyer can then choose to buy your stock at any time before this expiration date once it is at or above the strike price.

You may be saying to yourself, hold on there Randall, that sounds like a losing proposition. Why would I want to rent out my stock only to see it being sold down the road? I thought that I was investing in the stock market to create wealth, not to be kicked out onto the sidelines.

Even if your stock is called away, that is sold at or prior to expiration, at your agreed upon strike price, you still can profit from the situation. Suffice it to say, that in an upcoming chapter, you'll learn how to properly structure each covered call position so that you can optimize your profitability when we discuss various strategies in great detail.

If you had set your strike price above your initial price paid for the stock you not only get to keep the premium from selling the call option, but you have also captured the capital gain of the stock rising from its initial price to the strike price. As well, you're positioned to take advantage of the next opportunity that presents itself.

I have found myself being exercised, that is to say having my stock called away, on a couple of occasions. Not only did I pick up both the call option premium and the capital gain on the stock price appreciation, within a week later I bought back into the same stock at a lower price point than my initial purchase price. Not a bad scenario at all. Just rinse and repeat when the opportunity presents itself. Could you see yourself benefiting from a similar scenario?

When you learn how to control your cash flow that is being generated from your options plays, you'll see the full potential behind selling covered calls. Now that we've touched briefly on how and why you should include dividend-producing stocks and covered call option plays in your investment portfolio, let's explore the FAST approach in greater detail, starting with the letter F, which stands for Finding great opportunities.

Chapter 5 - Finding Wonderful Stocks

Focus Questions:
1. How can I find great stocks?
2. What megatrends should I keep my eye on?
3. Which sources of information will help me find potential stocks?
4. What stock screening tools could I use?

Having now given you a quick overview of why you should incorporate dividend-paying stocks and covered call writing into your overall cash flow investment plan, let's take a detailed look at each aspect of FAST starting with the letter F for Finding potential candidates.

Use a Top-Down Approach:
Every stock investor would love to own a portfolio of stocks that has the greatest potential for consistent capital appreciation over time with limited downside risk. The challenge is in knowing which stocks to place on your watch list of top candidates. Here's one stock selection strategy to help you with the decision-making process.

By looking initially at what the overall economy is doing, you can narrow down those sectors or industries that offer the best growth prospects over the next couple of years. Why just a few years? The harsh reality is that the economy expands and contracts on average every 4-5 years. So, trying to make realistic growth projections for time periods greater than 2-3 years becomes extremely challenging for any investor.

A short-term top-down approach takes a macro (or bird's eye) view of the economy. Imagine being a forester who focuses on looking at the health of the overall forest before checking out the individual trees that can be harvested. Your initial goal is to place more emphasis on identifying market trends that will support certain sectors and then select those industries that will benefit from the trends. Once you have a feel for the overall market, you can drill down and select the best businesses in each industry or sector. Good, so far?

Here are three questions that help me get started in assessing the current market environment:

Question #1: Is the economy expanding, contracting or experiencing a recession?

This information is readily available from government sources, as well as from several major financial websites like Yahoo Finance, MSN Money or Morningstar. Look for official announcements indicating the state of affairs of the economy.

Question #2: What is the primary trend in the stock market?

By looking at a technical chart of a broad index such as the S&P 500 you can assess whether or not recent market conditions have been neutral (as in 2011), bullish (a positive outlook) or bearish (a negative outlook).

Question #3: What is the interest rate trend?

If interest rates are rising there may be competition from high-quality fixed-income instruments (like bonds) that may impact how money flows into and out of the stock market. More importantly, higher interest rates affect economic sectors differently.

Businesses listed on the major stock market exchanges can be loosely grouped into 11 economic sectors of like businesses representing key areas of the economy. Examples of some specific observations that you can use to your advantage in screening for a promising economic sector of stocks are:

    1.   A low inflation rate trend will benefit the retailing industry.

2. A high inflation rate trend benefits the mining sector.
3. A slowdown in consumer spending affects the consumer staples sector the least.
4. A strengthening economy benefits the consumer discretionary sector which tends to be cyclical in nature.
5. A slowing economy is beneficial for health care and consumer staples, which are known as defensive stocks in a bad economy.
6. Rapidly increasing global debt has a negative impact on the financial sector.

Once you have identified in which sectors to concentrate your efforts, you can then start screening for those top-notch businesses that are the market leaders in their respective industries.

Megatrends to Keep Your Eye on:
In keeping in line with our top-down approach, here are 7 global trends that could provide you with some potential stock investing opportunities.

Trend #1: Mobile Internet.
This past decade, world demand for cell phones capable of accessing the internet is skyrocketing. This is especially so in nations that do not have a strong landline infrastructure, such as China and India. Look for companies that either produce the phones or develop the technology that is integrated into each phone.

Trend #2: Senior Healthcare.
The over 50 crowd is the fastest growing sector of the American population. As this segment of the population ages they will require more services related to health care. Of particular note are the pharmaceutical companies and drug retailers who should see

steadily increasing demand for their products, even should a recession hit. Of particular note, is the growth potential of the cannabis industry as more and more jurisdictions worldwide move to legalizing marijuana.

Trend #3: Precious Metals.

Gold and silver do especially well in times of great geopolitical unrest and inflation. Should things continue to heat up in Europe and the Middle East count on the demand for gold and silver to increase. There is currently a notable demand in India, China, Russia and the Middle East for the shiny stuff. Whether you decide to pick up physical gold or invest in shares of a growing producer is a matter of personal preference. They both have their inherent advantages.

Trend #4: Alternative Energy.

As technology advances so does the feasibility of integrating more and more green energy solutions into our current power grid. With nuclear reactor scares in the Ukraine and Japan, many nations are leaning towards other alternative sources of power. Companies to explore are those that specialize in wind turbines, solar panels, fuel cells, geothermal heating and the harnessing of ocean currents.

Trend #5: Oil & Gas.

Despite an increase in the green movement globally, oil and gas will continue to be a major play for investors moving into the future. This commodity is not going to get any cheaper with time. Most of the "easy" oil has been tapped out. Companies that should do well in the future are those specializing in major oil drilling. As well, should the price of a barrel of oil steadily increase over time, Canada's oil sands may be worth checking out.

Trend #6: Building Materials.

Two of the largest consumers of building materials are China and India whose economies will continue to grow over the next decade. Companies that should see a steady growth in sales as a result of increasing demand for construction material are those producing goods such as copper, steel and wood. Also look at companies whose job is to move building material globally either by rail or ship.

Trend #7: Counter Terrorism.

With continued global political instability, we will see more developed nations spending considerable sums of money on tracking, monitoring and detecting terrorist activity. Those companies that specialize in counter terrorism technology should fare well in the coming years.

There you have it - a snapshot of several megatrends that should help point you in the right direction for potential investment plays.

10 Great Sources of Information to Help You Find Potential Stocks:

Once you have an idea as to which of the 11 economic sectors or top industries to explore, your next step is to identify potential investment candidates. Here are 10 tips that will save you some time conducting your initial research in discovering those profitable best-of-breed businesses that can move you closer to reaching your point of financial freedom.

Tip #1: Buy what you know.

The first source taps into your passions, skills and interests. In order to invest confidently in any one business, it's important for that particular business or industry to have some personal meaning to you. The stronger your personal connection to the industry in terms of first-hand knowledge and experience, the greater your chances of selecting a wonderful stock that you're willing to follow up on.

A couple of reflective questions to ask yourself are: What hobbies do you pursue that might give you a greater insight into a particular business or industry? And in which businesses do you spend your money?

Here's a little exercise to help you identify the types of businesses that have meaning to you:
1. Draw three interlocking circles (like the Olympic rings) that for a triangle on a sheet of paper.
2. Write down everything you are PASSIONATE about in one circle.
3. Jot down your TALENTS in the second circle.
4. Identify what either makes you MONEY or that you spend your money on in the third circle.
5. Look for key words that show up in more than one circle.

These words have greater meaning to you and make looking for related businesses easier. Your goal is to try to find as many relevant connections as possible to those types of businesses that you might understand better than others. The next step is to brainstorm a list of those potential industries and specific companies that you would enjoy researching based on your key words.

Tip #2: Check Out Free Websites.
Your 2nd source of information is the stock screening tools available on several free websites such as Yahoo Finance and MSN Money. Using the search capabilities of each site you can find potential industries that might be of interest and then drill down to come up with a list of businesses that should have meaning to you.

Tip #3: National Business News Channels.

The 3rd source of potential stock picks is available on business news channels like CNBC, PBS or your favorite national business news station. Sometimes you can get great leads on businesses to consider in your initial investigation by watching TV programs like WealthTrack on PBS, Jim Cramer's Mad Money or Fast Money on CNBC. Jot down the names of those potential companies that tweak your interest. Something to consider, right?

Tip #4: The Print Media.

The 4th great source is through the print media. Books, magazines & newspapers are another source of potential companies to explore. Before buying any book or magazine or thinking about subscribing to any newspaper, save yourself some money by checking out the various sources at your local library, book store or magazine rack.

A few of books to check out are **John Slatter's The 100 Best Aggressive Stocks You Can Buy**, **Jim Cramer's Getting Back to Even** or **Charles Carlson's The Little Book of Big Dividends**. You'll find a more extensive list of books to explore at the end of the book in the Resource section.

There are a multitude of magazines to choose from, such as Forbes, Fortune, Smart Money and Smart Investor. As far as newspapers, check out the Wall Street Journal or The New York Times for ideas.

Tip #5: Stock Investment Websites.

The 5th source of potential stock picks is to see what words of wisdom you can gleam from various stock investment blogs and websites. There is a lot of free information available on the web.

You can also check out paid subscription sites such as the American Association of Independent Investors, Motley Fool's Stock Advisor, The Street.com or Investor's Business Daily for suggestions.

Tip #6: Watch your local TV newscast.

This tip piggy backs off the above one. Many TV stations look for opportunities to showcase local businesses that are breaking onto the international scene with new technological advances or state of the art products and services that appeal to a global market. Look for those news reports that highlight growing national franchises with a local home base. You may be able to tap into that hometown advantage by getting a different perspective about a company through the local news.

Unfortunately, the morning news is where they start by saying "good morning" and proceed to tell you why it isn't. Go easy on vegging in front of the boob tube.

Tip #7: Check the business section of your local newspaper.

Look for businesses that are being profiled because they are able to benefit from recent government contracts, positive changes within their industry or growing global trends for their products and services. As well, keep an eye out for those national businesses that are consistently advertising not only their products or services but also their reach and influence into the international arena.

Tip #8: Keep your eyes open for new store openings.

As you're making your way throughout your home town, pay attention to the signs announcing new store or factory openings. Are any major malls currently expanding to accommodate growing national franchises? This may get you thinking about the businesses that you should place on your personal investment watch list.

Tip #9: Pay attention to billboard advertising.

During your commute to and from work, make a mental note as to which major corporations are advertising frequently on billboards. Who are the businesses that have been consistently promoting their brand awareness? This insight may help to identify companies that are aggressively marketing their goods and services and may be poised to expand more globally.

Tip #10: Observe shopping behavior in the local mall.

One of my favorite strategies for finding great stocks has been to walk through shopping malls with the express intent of analyzing consumer behavior. Which stores seem to always be busy no matter what time or day of the week?

For example, I was able to see the potential of sporting goods retailer Lulu Lemon Athletics well before the stock price reflected the consumer buying trend that was unfolding for the company. Another retailer that caught my attention in the same way in 2010 was Apple. Coincidentally, the company had a great rally in the stock market throughout most of 2011 and into 2012.

Once you have identified several businesses that have the potential to become major international players, your next step is to place them on your watch list, which can be a simple list of the stocks on an electronic spreadsheet. I've found that by generating a list of about 40 interesting prospects, I can whittle this down by further investigating the company's growth potential. This is the 2nd step in FAST: assessing those watch list stocks.

Before we delve into assessing the potential of a particular stock, let's take a look at several stock screening tools that will make your job easier in compiling a list of potential candidates.

Nine Stock Screening Tools to Explore:

Here are nine popular websites that offer free and paid screening tools for the retail investor. This is by no means an exhaustive list of tools available online. Please take a moment to visit a few of these sites to get a better sense of what is available. As well, take some time to play around with the various stock screening tools so that you'll have a better idea as to what works best for you. Your primary objective is to quickly come up with a list of potential businesses that have solid growth prospects.

Tool #1: Big Safe Dividend Formula.

For top quality dividend-paying stocks, take a look at author **Charles Carlson's** website: http://www.bigsafedividends.com

At the site, he has up-to-date dividend ratings for dividend-paying stocks from the S&P 1500 Index. These stocks are ranked according to his proprietary Big Safe Dividend or BSD Formula, which is based on two premises:

- A company cannot pay a dividend if it doesn't have the money to pay dividends.
- You need to choose stocks that have attractive total-return potential, not just dividend return.

Carlson's formula is based on two data points:

1. Payout ratio:

This is the percentage of profits paid out as dividends. The higher the ratio, the more danger the company is in of reducing or eliminating the dividend if problems develop.

2. Overall Quadrix score:

Quadrix is a stock ranking system of more than 4000 stocks based on more than 100 variables across six categories, namely:

1. Momentum due to earnings, cash flow and sales growth.
2. Quality in terms of return on investment, return on equity and return on assets.
3. Value assessments based on price to sales, price to earnings, and price to book ratios.
4. Financial strength in terms of debt levels.
5. Earnings estimates.
6. Relative stock price performance to the industry and overall market.

Rest assured that we'll cover each of these parameters in the next chapter on assessment tools, okay? The best way to use the BSD formula is to focus your initial research on stocks that have a Quadrix score in the upper quartile of the percentile ranking system. This would mean looking at those stocks scoring above 75 out of 100.

Carlson has two versions of his BSD formula. His advanced formula uses 10 factors to evaluate dividend stability and growth. Should you start your screening process with the advanced formula, look for scores above 80 out of 100. You'll also find information about dividend payment schedules and current dividend yields on his site. **Carlson** is a big advocate for using the payout ratio as your primary screening tool. I tend to concur. Start by looking for stocks with low payout ratios. Many novice investors screen for high dividend yield stocks only to be disappointed as the dividend is cut or eliminated because the payout level is unsustainable. I like this particular site for finding stocks for my core holdings since it uses roughly the same screening criteria that I use when finding best-of-breed businesses.

Tool #2: Value Line.

http://www.valueline.com

The Value Line Investment Survey is most famous for its time-tested Ranking Systems for Timeliness, which ranks approximately 1,700 stocks relative to each other for price performance during the next six to 12 months, along with safety. Stocks are ranked from 1 to 5, with 1 being the highest ranking. Start by screening for No. 1 for Timeliness and Safety. This will give you an initial list of 100 stocks to filter through. An annual subscription to Value Line Investor 600 is currently $199. You may also want to check out your local library to see if they carry the newsletter for free.

Tool #3: Morningstar.

https://www.morningstar.com

The Morningstar 5-Star Rating System for stocks uses a business-centered approach. The rating compares a stock's current price with their analyst's estimate of the stock's fair value. The estimate is based on the present value of the company's future cash flows and does not factor in stock price momentum, investor sentiment or other nonfinancial factors. The Morningstar Rating System identifies stocks that are trading at a discount or at a premium to their fair values.

Morningstar has one of the best stock screening tools on the market. After signing up for a free account you'll have access to both predefined and custom screens. Initially screen for stocks that have a 5-star rating.

If you want to tap into the full potential of Morningstar's wealth of research, you'll need to subscribe to Morningstar's Premium Membership Service. You can sign up for a free 2-week trial period on the Morningstar website. Fortunately, many online discount brokers provide access to many of the stock screening tools and reports offered by Morningstar. Check with your online broker to see what might be available.

Tool #4: American Association of Individual Investors.

https://www.aaii.com/stock-screens/
This website is chock full of helpful ideas as well as an entire section devoted to stock screening.

The purpose of AAII's Stock Screen area is to provide members with access to a wide range of stock strategies and investment approaches. The stock screens are updated monthly and cover over 60 stock investment strategies as well as the companies that pass each screen.

The basic annual membership to the AAII is $49. Membership privileges include:
1. 12 Issues of the *AAII Journal*.
2. AAII Model Stock, Mutual Fund, and ETF Portfolios.
3. Yearly Tax Planning Guide.
4. Access to Local Chapter Meetings (over 50 nationwide).
5. 60 On-Line Stock Screens.

The American Association of Individual Investors is a non-profit education publisher that has been successfully aiding do-it-yourself investors for over 35 years.

Tool #5: Yahoo! Finance.

http://screener.finance.yahoo.com/newscreener.html
Yahoo Finance allows you to create your own screens with over 150 different stock screening criteria. This is a good free stock screen to use for simple screens.

Tool #6: Market Watch.

http://www.marketwatch.com/tools/stockresearch/screener

Not only do you have access to a simple stock screening tool, you can also watch current videos organized into the various economic sectors. These videos provide insights into what is transpiring in each of these sectors.

Tool #7: CNBC Stock Screener
http://www.cnbc.com/stock-screener/
CNBC offers both predefined and custom screening tools. Check out their simple predefined screens for:
1. High Quality High Dividends which uses an income investing approach. or
2. Large Cap Growth which uses a growth investing approach to stock selection.

Tool #8: MSN Money.
https://www.msn.com/en-us/money/stockscreener/
Stock Scouter is a 10-point stock rating system that ranks the stocks according to preset criteria. I have used this tool as an initial starting point for some of my own research.

Tool #9: The Blue Collar Investor.
https://www.thebluecollarinvestor.com/
Bar none, this is the next best thing to winning the lottery. The Blue Collar Investor is one of my favorite screening and educational sites for cash flow investors. *Alan Ellman* has been successfully using covered call strategies for over a decade. His premium membership is geared towards the do-it-yourself stock investor wanting to capitalize on using covered call option strategies with market leaders. You'll receive weekly reports for:
- The top stocks to write (sell) covered calls on.
- The top dividend-producing stocks. and
- The top ETF's with option contracts.

A 1st month premium trial is $19.95 and $49.95 each month thereafter. What I've found is that by using this tool, I'm able to shave hours of research off my investing. Not only that, the stock picks are selected specifically with covered call strategies in mind, which is an added bonus. Something to consider investing in, down the road, wouldn't you agree?

And did I mention that going through specific option examples is beyond the scope of this book? Well, *Ellman's* site offers a plethora of short, informative videos on how to execute various strategies. You can access this wealth of knowledge on this site or on his You Tube channel The Blue Collar Investor.

There you have it. You now have an idea as to where to look for potential opportunities that you could put onto your watch list. Whether or not you sign up for a premium stock screening service from one of the providers mentioned, have some fun exploring the free sites before committing to one or several paid services.

Should you like to experiment with some basic screening criteria to plug into one of the tools here are a couple of options:

Growth Stock Criteria:
Price ≥ 10
Market Cap ≥ $1 billion
PEG ≤ 1.5
Debt/ Equity ≤ 50%
Earnings Growth Past 5 Years ≥ 15 %
Sales Growth Estimate This Year ≥ 15 %

Dividend Stock Criteria:
Price ≥ 10
Market Cap ≥ $1 billion
Dividend Yield ≥ 3%

Earnings Growth Estimate Next 5 Years ≥ 7.5%
ROE ≥ 10%

Now that you have a better idea as to how to find potential candidates, let's narrow down your watch list by looking at assessing the growth potential of each prospect. To do so, I'll share some basic selection criteria to help you assess the viability of your picks. Are you ready for a well-deserved break? Thought so.

Chapter 6 - Assessing Potential Stocks

Focus Questions:
1. What variables should you use to assess a company's merits?
2. Which criteria specific to dividend-paying stocks should I consider using?
3. Why are growth rates so important?
4. What are some simple ways to calculate growth rates?
5. How can economic moats help me make money?

The identification and assessment of potential stocks can be a tedious process. Wherever possible, the smart cash flow investor will use those free or inexpensive tools that make the selection process faster and easier.

The extent of research and effort that you'll put in boils down to three factors:
- How much time you have to realistically do your due diligence.
- Whether or not your stock will be held long-term as an investment, such as a dividend-paying stock, or short-term as a cash flow trade as in the case of a monthly covered call.
- Your personal preference as to how much money you could allocate to tap into the speed and convenience offered by subscription sites like The Blue Collar Investor.

My intent in the last chapter was to showcase several stock screening tools thereby giving you some options that you can access. Once you have screened for some potential stock candidates and placed them on your personal watch list, the choice will be up to you to either drill down deeper and assess the quality of each particular opportunity on your own using the assessment criteria described in this chapter or use a paid service that will provide you with some strong possibilities.

My advice to every upcoming investor is to initially learn how to use the assessment criteria as part of your overall selection process. Once you understand how each particular factor helps you identify those best-of-breed industry leaders that offer you the greatest upside potential, then you can begin to streamline your selection process as you become more familiar with what each factor has to offer. Does that make sense?

I can also offer these words of wisdom that may help guide you in your decision-making process:

1. The longer your holding period for your stock pick the more effort you should put into the assessment process. For example, if you are looking for a quality dividend-paying stock that you would like to hang onto for at least one year, then take the time to check out the business thoroughly.
2. The greater the reward and risk involved in the selection of a particular investment strategy the more time you should spend assessing the upside potential of the stock you're considering.

Let's take a look at some of the personal favorite assessment criteria used by many of the successful stock investors and educators in today's marketplace.

Top 10 Assessment Criteria for Best of Breed Businesses:

You may have noticed that when you screened for a particular type of stock several criteria were used in the selection process for finding great stocks. This is critical to identifying fundamentally sound businesses with upside growth potential.

According to **James O'Shaughnessy** in his book **What Works on Wall Street: The Classic Guide to the Best-Performing Investment Strategies of All Time**, "using several value factors together in a composited value factor offers much better and more consistent returns than using individual value factors on their own." What **O'Shaughnessy** is saying is that a multi-variable screening approach provides the investor with a higher quality list of potential best-of-breed businesses from which to choose.

Let me jump right in with a list of the top 10 indicators that I like to use for both finding great stocks and assessing their potential. This list is by no means an exhaustive or exclusive list. It has served me and other cash flow investors well in identifying market leaders who are top-notch businesses. I've based my list on what several of the top investment experts have used in their selection process. By looking at recent best practices in the stock investment industry, I was able to drill down and create a short list of the most popular criteria for finding wonderful businesses for your stock portfolio.

Without further ado, here are the top 10 indicators that many of the top dogs like to use for finding great stocks:

1. Payout ratio for dividend-paying stocks being less than 60%.
2. Return on invested capital (ROIC) being greater than 10%.
3. Book value per share growth rate (BVPS) of at least 10%.
4. Earnings per share growth rate (EPS) being greater than 10%.
5. Revenue or sales growth rate greater than 10%.
6. Cash flow growth rate of 10%.
7. Debt-to-equity ratio (D/E) which should be low and preferably less than 0.5.
8. Price-to-earning-to-growth ratio (PEG) of less than 1.0.

9. Price-to-sales ratio (P/S) which should be low, preferably under 1.0.
10. Relative strength index (RSI) should be high for momentum plays within a range of 60 to 80.

All of the "growth rates" should be consistent over a minimum 5-year period. In general, what I look for is consistent growth in earnings over a period of 5 to 7 years and with the capital being generated being put to good use by the management to grow the business.

Now that you have an idea as to which factors you can use in your assessment process let's take a look at how each of these 10 factors can be used in our assessment process.

Selecting Dividend Stocks for the FAST Approach:

Dividend stocks tend to be the least volatile class of stocks in the market. They continue to be favorite picks among novice investors, retirees and more conservative investors in general. However, knowing which stocks have the potential to provide a safe return can prove to be daunting for many investors. Dividend-paying companies have normally experienced their biggest growth spurt and don't require all of their cash flows to fund their expansion. Such companies are confident that their future profitability will support a dividend payment and are thus inclined to return some of those profits back to the shareholders.

After having read numerous books on the subject of dividend stock investing, I came to realize that there were four criteria that the majority of the authors referenced in selecting top dividend-paying stocks. I'll start by giving you an overview of the various criteria to consider, specific to dividend-paying stocks. Then we'll continue with the remaining nine indicators applicable to any stock. Sound good so far?

To start, the most popular criteria to use that will help you in your decision-making process for selecting dividend stocks and that we'll use as guidelines are the following:

Factor #1: Payout Ratio Test.
The payout ratio looks at the percentage of the company's net earnings that is paid out to the shareholders as dividends. A lower ratio signals a healthier or safer dividend income.

Looking at our growth dividend companies; these tend to have payout ratios under 30 to 40% because they prefer investing any net earnings in their future growth and thus choose to hold onto much of their excess cash for internal growth purposes. As for income dividend companies, payout ratios fall into the 30 to 70% range. As a general rule of thumb, look for payout ratios around 50 to 60 %. Ratios between 70% and 100% may be unsustainable with the dividend being cut or eliminated as a result.

Real Estate Investment Trusts, Master Limited Partnerships and Royalty Trusts that are by law required to pay back the majority of their net earnings in the form of dividends usually have payout ratios in excess of 90%. Unfortunately, the disadvantage of being more vulnerable to dividend cuts and having no preferential tax treatment, as with most other dividend-paying companies is a deterrent for using these investment vehicles for our purposes.

Charles Carlson in his book *The Little Book of Big Dividends* places a high priority on the payout ratio in assessing the merits of top dividend-paying stocks.

Other Factors Worth Considering:
Although not part of the overall top 10 most referenced criteria, three other factors that are worth considering in your dividend

selection process once you have drilled down to a handful of potential candidates are the following:

Dividend Yield.

The dividend yield is the percentage of the share's stock price that you get back every year from dividend payments. It is calculated by dividing the stock's annual dividend yield by its share price. For example, if you bought a dividend stock that has an annual dividend payout of $1 and you paid $20 per share, then the yield would be: $1 / $20 = 0.05 or a return of 5%. This percentage rate of return is the quickest way to determine how much money you will initially earn from each potential stock pick.

Generally speaking, the higher the percentage, the better the return on your initial purchase. Keep in mind that the yield you receive can change over time decreasing as the stock price increases; assuming that there has not been a change in the annual payout amount.

We can loosely group dividend-paying companies into two categories - those that are growth oriented and those that are income oriented. Growth companies usually have high profitability that can provide you with both capital appreciation of the stock and income gains from dividends. In today's economic environment, growth dividend companies have yields ranging from 2 to 4% while income dividend companies have yields of 4 to 6%. These tend to be the sweet spots for both categories.

In addition, growth companies tend to have high dividend growth rates of 10 to 12%; whereas, income dividend companies fall into the 6 to 10% range. The growth rate of the dividend is an important factor to take into consideration when we build our investment portfolio.

Historical Range.

In order to find high-quality dividend stocks, look for companies that raise their dividends consistently over a twenty to thirty-year period, especially in the midst of a poor economy. By comparing the current yield to the historical range, you can determine if it's significantly higher and therefore presents a good buying opportunity. To find the historical yield, check out a free site such as Yahoo Finance and click on "Historical Data".

Free Cash Flow Test.

Similar to the payout ratio, you can look at the company's free cash flow for the quarter or the year in comparison to the quarterly or annual dividend payout.

The free cash flow is found in the company's cash flow statement. Most free financial websites reporting on the stock market have this information readily available. The free cash flow should adequately cover the payment of the dividend to the shareholders. Once again, look for an ideal ratio of around 50 to 60%.

As you may have already ascertained, the previous four criteria are particular to selecting dividend-paying stocks. Let's now continue with the nine popular assessment criteria for all stocks starting with growth rates.

The 5 Key Growth Rates continued:

A common question that I am asked is: Which financial numbers do I need to listen to in order to confirm the strength of a business?

Ideally, you want to be able to use just a handful of indicators that help you determine whether you can both trust and predict that the business can deliver double-digit returns in the future. We want to keep the process as simple as possible. We also want to be able to compare rates of change as opposed to the raw numbers. Monitoring rates of change goes hand-in-hand with the concept of increasing the velocity of your money. Some of the most popular indicators and the top five that I personally use in my assessment process are:

Factor #2: *Return on Investment Capital (ROIC).*

The ROIC is the rate of return a business makes on the cash it invests every year. The ROIC is a measure of how effective a company uses its own and borrowed money invested in its operations. I place greater weight on this fundamental ratio as it tells the investor how effective the business is in using invested capital. This ratio is a strong predictor that the business has a competitive advantage in its industry.

Factor #3: *Equity or Book Value per Share Growth Rate (BVPS).*

The BVPS is what a business would be worth if it's no longer a business. This would be the liquidation value or book value of the company. The raw number is not important since factory-type businesses can vary immensely with intellectual property businesses. It's the rate of equity growth that is key in comparing businesses. We're looking for businesses that are able to accumulate a growing surplus over time and not spending excessive funds to build new capital-intensive projects.

Factor #4: *Earnings per Share Growth Rate.*

The EPS indicates how much the business is profiting per share of ownership. The EPS is often found as the last line on the income statement. However, we're more concerned with the growth rate, which we'll either quickly calculate on our own or find in certain financial websites reporting on business fundamentals.

Factor #5: Sales or Revenue Growth Rate.

The sales growth rate represents the total dollars the business took in from selling its products and services. It's usually located on the top line of the income statement.

Factor #6: Free Cash Flow Growth Rate.

Free cash flow is an indicator as to whether a business is growing its cash with profits or if the profits are only on paper.

Ideally, all of the growth rates should be equal to or greater than 10 percent per year for the last 5, 3 and 1 year. Having at least these three numbers gives you a better sense of how the company is growing over a period of time. Fundamental to all of the numbers is consistency. We want all the numbers going up or at least staying the same.

I realize that this quick overview of the top 5 growth rates just gives you a smattering of what to assess. Self-made stock investment millionaire **Phil Town** pioneered the approach of using 5 fundamental growth rates to find wonderful businesses at attractive prices. He provides a detailed step-by-step process for assessing the merits of any stock in his books **Rule #1** and **Payback Time**. Can you see how these resources could make your learning that much easier?

Factor #7: Debt-to-Equity Ratio.

The debt-to-equity ratio is a simple measure of how much the company owes in relation to how much it owns. It's calculated by dividing the total liabilities by the net equity. This ratio is easy to find on most financial websites. It should be low and preferably less than 0.5.

You can also look at a company's balance sheet to determine the total amount of debt coming due over the next few years. If there is a great deal of debt, dividends from dividend-paying companies may be slashed in order to ensure paying off any bond holders first. Here's a tip. Do a quick check is to see if the long-term debt of the company can be paid off in less than 3 years with the current free cash flow or net earnings. This gives you a margin of safety in assessing the extent of debt on the company's books. Ideally, this should be zero thus enabling the business to readily respond to drastic changes in the economy. However, those businesses capable of paying off debt within a 3-year window are still good prospects to consider.

Factor #8: PEG ratio.

A helpful indicator when comparing two or more like businesses together is the PEG ratio. The PEG is the Price-to-Earnings Multiple (P/E) divided by its earnings growth rate. It is an indicator of growth at a reasonable price, or what the stock investment industry calls GARP.

The PEG is a great way to identify growth stocks that are still selling at a good price. The lower the PEG the better, since you're getting more earnings growth for every dollar invested. As a rule of thumb, healthy companies have PEG rates less than 1, whereas a PEG rate over 2 is expensive.

The PEG ratio was championed by investment guru **Peter Lynch** who generated an annualized return of 29.8 % from 1977 to 1990 from Fidelity's Magellan Fund while the S&P 500 had an average return of 15.8 %.

Factor #9: Price-to-Sales Ratio.

The price-to-sales ratio was promoted by investment guru **Ken Fisher** back in the 80's. **Fisher** believed that earnings can be more volatile in the traditional P/E ratio as opposed to sales which tend to rarely decline in good companies. The PSR is calculated by dividing the stock price per share by the total sales per share. This ratio can help indicate if you are paying too much for the company's stock based on its sales. This is a useful indicator when assessing retailers.

The general rule of thumb is that the lower the PSR the better. Cyclical retailers with a PSR between 0.4 and 0.8 are good investment candidates. A cyclical stock is one that does better when the economy is doing well and people have more discretionary money to spend. Noncyclical and technology stocks with a PSR between 0.75 and 1.5 also offer good value for investors.

Factor #10: Relative Strength Index.
The RSI measures the velocity and magnitude of directional price movements in a stock. It's most typically used on a 14-day timeframe. The indicator is measured on a scale from 0 to 100, with high and low levels marked at 80 and 20, respectively.

I've included this one technical indicator of stock momentum into the mix for screening potential candidates. The reason becomes apparent based on **James O'Shaughnessy** comment in his book **What Works on Wall Street** that "we find that relative strength is among the only pure growth factors that actually beats the market consistently, by a wide margin."

O'Shaughnessy says to "buy stocks with the best relative strength, but understand that their volatility will continually test your emotional endurance." When we explore momentum plays later in this book, you'll see the power behind this technical indicator. Start your initial screening by looking for stocks that have an RSI above 50 and below 80 on a 100-point scale. So far, so good? Moving along to what specific steps to take for your assessment process.

An Overview of the Stock Assessment Process:

Now that we have an idea as to some of the specific indicators that we can use for assessing the money-making potential of any business, it might be the time to step back and provide a quick overview of how that process will unfold.

There are three key steps to follow when picking potential stocks for your investment portfolio. Your primary objective is to analyze several businesses and determine which ones have the greatest upside potential for growth. In essence, before you commit any of your hard-earned cash to any stock purchase, you'll be doing an in-depth best-of-breed analysis of several businesses. This analysis takes into account the following three steps:

Step #1: Compare the fundamentals of the business over a minimum 5-year period of time. Fundamentals refer to the rate of growth of sales, income, and equity in comparison to the on-going expenses and liabilities. We've just covered ten of the most popular indicators used by many professional investors to help them select fundamentally sound stocks. Ideally, you're looking for businesses with a long track record of consistently growing owner/ shareholder equity year to year.

Step #2: Determine the type and extent of the competitive advantage or economic moat that the business has created that sets it apart from its competition. We'll explore seven types of economic moats in a moment.

Step #3: Assess the management's focus and compensation. You're looking for CEO's that are passionate about their work and the importance they place on creating real long-term sustainable value for their shareholders. Look for management teams that are fairly compensated for their efforts as opposed to the few who rip off unsuspecting shareholders with outrageous bonuses.

Since we've already explored the key fundamentals that you should consider when finding and sizing up potential candidates, we'll delve into how 7 different types of economic moats help you make money in the markets. Sound like a plan, Sam?

7 Types of Economic Moats to Help You Make Money:
There are many factors you should consider when choosing those top-notch businesses that have great growth potential and are capable of generating substantial profits for you over the years. So, how important is it that a company has a well-established economic moat? The short answer: crucial.

An economic moat refers to the notion that the business has some durable competitive advantage, not unlike a moat that protects a castle from attack. The wider the moat the easier it is to fend off attackers. Finding a business with a wide moat is key to finding a successful business to own; the wider the moat, the more predictable its future 5 to 10 years down the road. Having a competitive edge, allows for a company to have a degree of predictability.

As an investor, you're looking for not only sustainable growth rates but also consistent growth in cash flow, equity and sales over a 3 to 5-year period of time. With increasing cash flow, profitability for both the business and you the shareholder arises. With increasing cash flow, a best-of-breed business can whether the ups and downs of the economic business cycle paying off debt when needed or investing capital for expanding into new markets. Wide moat companies are also protected from inflation since their "monopolistic position" enables them to raise prices at will.

Here are seven types of economic moats to look for in a potential business:

Moat #1: Brand – a product or service you're willing to pay more for because you know and trust it. Companies like Disney and Nike have good brand moats.

Moat #2: Secret - a patent, copyright or trade secret that makes competition difficult or illegal. Examples of these companies are 3M, Pfizer and Apple.

Moat #3: Toll - having exclusive control of a market through government approval or licensing thus being able to charge a "toll" for accessing that product or service. Such businesses as PG & E, a utility company and Time Warner a media business fit the mold.

Moat #4: Switching - being too much trouble to switch to another provider due to the high monetary and time costs. Microsoft and H & R Block are two good examples.

Moat #5: Low Price - products priced so low no one can compete because they enjoy massive economies of scale due to a huge market share. Home Depot, Costco and Wal-Mart are examples of businesses that have used pricing to establish an economic advantage.

Moat #6: Network Effect - the ability to quickly dominate a network of end-users by being first in the market. EBay was the first online auction business to dominate the North American market.

Moat #7: Unique Corporate Culture - a way of doing business that would be difficult to duplicate in another business environment. Southwest Airlines benefited from this type of economic moat in the early years.

You need not find a company with multiple moats to consider it to be a potential investment candidate. It should have one moat that seems hardest to cross and one that is sustainable long-term. And how do you identify an economic moat? The establishment of a viable economic moat shows up in the fundamentals. Companies with consistently high growth rates of over 10% per year in return on invested capital, sales, equity and free cash over many years are the ideal candidates.

Top 4 Mistaken Economic Moats:

Real economic moats are structural characteristics of a business that provide the investor with a degree of predictability of the sustained cash flow that will be generated over many years, if not decades. However, some investors may incorrectly mistake certain characteristics of a business as being some sort of economic advantage. The top four mistaken moats to watch out for are:

Mistake #1: Great products.

Unfortunately, great products come and go, especially if the product is commodity based and can be easily replicated. Having a great product does not provide a long-term assurance that the competition won't come in with a newer, sexier, cheaper version in a few months' time. If it's easy for the consumer to switch from one particular product to another, beware of this potential business as an investment opportunity.

Mistake #2: Strong market share.

In the short term, a business may dominate a particular market with their product or service. This may give you the false sense of security that they have somehow created a monopoly. High market share can dwindle very quickly as more competition enters the marketplace.

Mistake #3: Great execution.

Businesses that pride themselves in being lean and mean can give the illusion that they have an advantage over the competition.

Being efficient is a fine business strategy, but it is not a sustainable competitive advantage unless it is based on some proprietary process that cannot be easily copied.

Mistake #4: Great management.

Although having passionate, shareholder-oriented management teams in place helps to create a wonderful business, it does not constitute being a sustainable advantage. Talented CEO's do help companies perform better. However, there is no long-term guarantee that a particular individual will be around in 3 or 5 years.

Is Management on Your Side?

Step 3 of your assessment process looks at who is running the company. As obvious as it may be, we want management to be on the side of the shareholder. However, this is not always the case. We've seen countless cases of incidents where the CEO did not have the shareholder's best interest at heart. Situations where the CEO is being paid hundreds of millions of dollars to run the company into the ground. Here are the top four qualities that you want to see in great CEO's:

- They are service-oriented as opposed to ego-oriented. Their focus is on serving the owners, the employees, the suppliers, and the customers.
- They are passionate about their work and the business they are managing.
- They never risk their honor to make a quick buck or ruin their reputation for power or prestige.
- They are driven to change the world for the better. They have big goals that inspire and motivate the organization.

How do you go about finding this information? Here are five ways to check out management without hiring a private eye:

- Google the CEO's name and read a few news articles in trade and business magazines and newspapers, such as Forbes, Fortune, Barron's, Success, the New York Times and the Wall Street Journal. What reputation does the CEO have in the business community?
- Check out the competition's websites and blogs for information about the manager and the company. What are they saying about their competition and the challenges in the market?
- Read the CEO's letter to shareholders and compare the growth rate numbers to what is being said. What is the tone of the letter? Look for CEO's who take responsibility for a bad year, as evidenced in the numbers, admits his or her mistakes and tells shareholders what he or she intends to do. These CEO's have integrity.
- To better understand a specific business, check out either the CEO's quarterly conference call held with analysts and recorded on the company's website or posted as a transcript of the call. A couple of hours of reading or listening every 3 months will teach you a whole lot about the CEO.
- Look at the Insider trading activity on MSN Money or Yahoo Finance. If company executives are unloading more than 30 percent of their stock all at once, this is not a good sign. As well, look for CEO's that are getting overpaid through stock options or outrageous perks in addition to their salary. Most free websites post this basic data.

Ask yourself, does the business have great Management? You must be confident that the people running the business are doing so as if they intend on being there for decades and not out to rip you off in the short term. Does that make sense?

Once you have explored a business's fundamentals, competitive advantage and management team you can use the same approach with that business's key competitors to determine who is the best-of-breed in that industry. By identifying and investing initially in only these best-of-breed companies across various sectors of the stock market, especially when they come on sale at attractive prices, you increase the likelihood that you'll build a successful investment portfolio.

All of this information can be recorded either in a notebook or in an Excel Spreadsheet. Although taking a little more time to set up, a spreadsheet affords the greatest future ease of use for both the calculations and updating information. This process has served me well in assessing potential candidates. It has helped me streamline the information flow so that I am more efficient, saving me time in the process.

Five Simple Ways to Calculate Growth Rates:
Are you wondering how you can determine or calculate the key growth rates that we discussed earlier? To wrap up this particular chapter let me share several ways that you can determine those key growth rates that you'll be using in your assessment process.

Unfortunately, most free web sites do not provide growth rates, just the raw data. Fortunately for us, by taking the time to determine these rates we position ourselves ahead of the majority of retail investors in assessing the true growth potential of any company. This is yet another example of how we are going to develop our competitive edge.

Yes. I do understand that this assessment process that I've walked you through, does initially require a time commitment. However, my goal (and yours as well for that matter) is to ensure that you don't lose any capital. This investigative approach helps minimize the chances of picking the wrong stock to hitch your wagon too.

Here are five different options that you can calculate the key growth rates that we'll be referring to in our assessment of potential businesses.

Option #1: Invest in Subscription Websites

As your stock investment portfolio grows, you may wish to invest in better quality information, than what is currently available for free, by purchasing a subscription to a stock analysis sites like Morningstar, Value Line, or The Blue Collar Investor. As previously mentioned subscription sites do save you a lot of time in finding and assessing potential candidates. This option is the easiest approach to identifying fundamentally sound businesses. Easy peasy, right?

You can also check out some of the free calculators that **Phil Town** has on his **Rule One Investing** website. Recall that **Phil** is a great proponent of using growth rates in finding wonderful stock picks.

Option #2: Access Growth Rates from Your Broker.

This option piggy backs off the previous one. Some brokerage firms will allow you to access additional information not currently available on many free websites. Please contact your broker to see if you have access to these ready-made calculations.

Option #3: Use Your Financial Calculator.

Are you a do-it-yourselfer? If you are adept at using a financial calculator, this may be a quick and easy way to calculate a variety of growth rates with varying time periods. To get started, all you need are a series of values over several years. Then you'll use these 4 keys on your calculator:

- PV (present value key) = your starting (oldest) value.
- FV (future value key) = most recent (current) value.
- N (number of years) = number of intervals from the starting value to the present value.
- CPT + %i (compute key followed by the percent interest key) = growth rate calculation.

Example using book value per share growth rate from 2007 to 2017:
Starting BVPS from 2007 = 8
Current BVPS from 2017 = 32
Number of intervals (years) = 2017 - 2007 = 10

Enter the following information on your calculator:
Type 8 and press the PV key
Type 32 and press the FV key
Type 10 and press the N key
Press the CPT key and then press the %i key
The result of 14.9 will appear.
This is the BVPS growth rate over a 10-year period.

Option #4: Create Your Own Excel Spreadsheet Formula.

If you feel ambitious and would like to create your own assessment spreadsheet, here are six simple steps to creating your own formula:
Step #1: In Excel, click on a cell and type =RATE(
You'll see the following formula
appear: RATE(nper,pmt,pv,[fv],[type],[guess])
Step #2: nper = number of periods. Subtract your current year (ex. 2017) from your starting year (ex. 2007) to get the number of periods (ex. 10). Input this number and then type a comma. The next item will go to bold.

Step #3: pmt = the payments each year. Since you are not doing payments, just type a comma.

Step #4: pv = the number you want to start with. Start by typing a *minus sign* and then enter your starting value. The minus sign tells the formula, that you have paid out an amount. Type a comma to move to the next parameter.

Step #5: [fv] = the number you end with. Enter your most current value. Just ignore [type] and [guess]. Then, type a *close parenthesis*.

Step #6: Press "Enter". Excel calculates the growth rate. There you have it. Just copy and paste the cell to set up formulas for each of the key growth rates.

Option #5: Mental Calculations of the Growth Rate.

And your final possible option is to perform the growth calculations in your head. Sometimes a little mental math is all that you need to perform in order to get an approximate value for a particular growth rate.

Many of you have heard of the rule of 72, which states that by dividing 72 by the number of years it takes to double your money, you end up with an approximation of the growth rate.

Using the same example as in Option #3, see how many times the initial BVPS value in 2007 doubles in 10 years to reach or slightly surpass the final BVPS value in 2017.

In other words, if the starting BVPS is 8 and the final BVPS is 32, how many times can you double 8 before reaching or slightly surpassing 32?

A BVPS of 8 doubles twice: once from 8 to 16 and then from 16 to 32.

Therefore, one double takes 5 years.

Using the "Rule of 72", divide the number of years it takes to double once into 72.

That is divide 72 by 5 which is approximately 14 ½. This is your percentage rate of growth.

You now have a good estimate of the annual growth rate over 10 years.

Whichever method you decide to employ when calculating growth rates, your primary goal as an investor should be to simplify the whole process. Choose the method that best suits your needs with this in mind.

In the next chapter, I'll share with you several cash flow strategies that'll empower you to become a better investor. Time for a break, wouldn't you agree?

Chapter 7 - Selecting the Right Strategies

Focus Questions:
1. How do I create a diverse portfolio of stock investments?
2. Which dividend investment strategy works well with the overall cash flow investment theme?
3. What two covered call strategies either produce income or emphasize growth?
4. Which covered call strategy should I use in a down-trending market?
5. How can I generate additional cash flow from my dividend stocks by layering on an option strategy?

In this chapter, we'll explore a handful of strategies that work well with an accelerated cash flow system. Are you fired up and ready to go? Do you know what I'm thinking? No. Neither do I; frightening isn't it?

The primary objective of this particular chapter is to not only walk you through cash flow strategies for dividend-paying stock and selling covered calls on stock that you own, but to also introduce you to the power of layering your positions.

The concept of layering positions starts with the premise that you'll build a portfolio of core stock holdings that provide a solid foundation from which to build your wealth. Once in place, another cash flow generation strategy is layered on top of the initial foundation. A common scenario is that of generating cash flow from a dividend-paying stock with an additional layer of selling covered calls providing another income stream; something that we'll explore later on. Sound good?

About Strategies:

Before we take a look at the handful of time-tested strategies outlined in this book, let's take a quick look at the obvious challenge many retail investors are faced with - that of picking which strategy to use.

There are an overwhelming number of popular investment strategies being used in the stock market today. Many experts tout that they have the perfect strategy that is the be-all and end-all to solving your investment woes. Many well-known investment authors who have been successful investing in the stock market often have a strong bias towards a particular strategy that better sells their services or investment product lines.

It's challenging to get an unbiased opinion about any particular investment strategy. Who can you really trust when many of them have a hidden agenda? The American Association of Individual Investors currently tracks over 60 investment strategies on their website. It's no wonder that most do-it-yourself retail investors are at a loss as to which approach to take.

The most important aspect about making money in the markets is to stick to a proven strategy over time. It becomes more of a factor the longer you work your specific strategy through good times and bad. Avoid adopting the attitude that if Plan A fails, you've got 25 more letters to choose from. The handful of strategies selected for accelerating your cash flow avoids this. They create opportunities to generate a significant stream of cash flow as well as increase the velocity of your money from one opportunity to a better one.

How to Create a Diverse Stock Portfolio:

Diversification means different things to different investors. Many mutual fund advisors tout that diversification is best achieved by buying an index or basket of 100 or more stocks through some type of fund. Others in the expert arena, such as **Jim Cramer** or **Phil Town** suggest holding a handful of stocks that have been personally selected.

So, how do you create a diverse portfolio of investments that provides both upside potential and downside protection of your wealth? For the avid stock investor, here are seven key factors to integrate into your investment portfolio in order to create an appropriate level of diversification:

Factor #1: Diversification Across Asset Classes.

As a lifelong investor, your ideal investment portfolio should contain not only stocks, but also investments from other asset classes.

By investing in other asset classes such as real estate rental property, commodities like oil and gold, systematized businesses that run on their own, or fixed-income investments like bonds, you spread out your risk across various investment markets. When one market is trending lower another unrelated one may be heading higher.

Investing in various asset classes creates a better balance in preserving your overall capital and should be one of your long-term investment objectives. Most self-made millionaires use a multi-faceted approach to wealth creation and so should you.

Although we're focusing on building wealth using the stock market as a vehicle, at some point in the future you may wish to explore other investment vehicles. Makes sense, right?

Factor #2: Diversification Within the Stock Market.

When you invest in the stock market, your portfolio may benefit from being invested in various groups of stocks that are classified by size or characteristics. For example, a core amount of your investment capital will be initially invested in dividend-paying large cap stocks, with a certain percentage of your capital being spread across the small or mid cap stock universe. Each group has its own unique characteristics that benefit from certain market or economic conditions. By the way, the expression "large cap" refers to large capitalization, which is another way of saying a large business.

At times, you may find that your investments in the small-cap universe will prove to be winners in a booming economy. At other times your dividend-paying stocks may out-perform the small or mid-cap stock universes. By diversifying your capital within the stock market, you can benefit from the changing tides that occur every 4 to 5 years.

Factor #3: Diversification Across the 11 Economic Sectors.

A popular way of grouping companies traded in the stock market has been to place them into 11 economic sectors based on the nature or purpose of the business. Examples of these economic sectors are the technology sector, consumer staples, energy, utilities and health care.

By allocating no more than 20% of your investment capital to any one of the 11 economic sectors provides you with better balance. As one economic sector goes out of favor with Mr. Market, another will quickly take its place. Spreading out your capital improves your odds of overall portfolio growth.

It stands to reason that once you have a number of good investment candidates you should be aware of how you allocate your capital across the 11 sectors.

Factor #4: Diversification Across the Globe.

God created the world, everything else is made in China. Although the U.S. has the most vibrant stock markets in the world, you should actively seek out companies that have a global exposure. This can be done with U.S. based companies that export more than 30% of their goods or services overseas or through ADR's, which are foreign companies that trade on U.S. exchanges.

Look for the tag ADR, which stands for American Depository Receipt, after the name of a company you're researching. Consider exposing yourself to Canadian companies in the financial sector or base materials. Canada has a commodity based economy and one of the strongest financial systems in the world.

Also take a look at the BRICS countries, Brazil, Russia, India, China and South Africa, whose growing middle class are buying more and more local products and services, not to mention those of the international players. To start with focus your attention on U.S. and Canadian companies with international exposure, as well as those foreign businesses listed as ADRs on the U.S. stock exchanges.

Factor #5: Diversification Across Time.

By investing on a regular basis, you're able to tap into opportunities as they present themselves. Having cash on hand to take advantage of miss pricings in the market allows you to buy into positions with a certain margin of safety.

Recall that it is the velocity of your money through the stock market from one investment to a better one that accelerates your wealth-building potential. The old adage of buy, hold and forget - no longer works in today's markets. You may be better served by moving your "dead money" into growth opportunities on a regular basis. Following me so far?

Factor #6: Diversification Across Investment Accounts.
Not all investment accounts are created equal. A few allow you to grow your investments tax-free, others defer the tax you pay and some offer better investment choices.

You should try to diversify your holdings across 3 general types of accounts because of the advantages and limitations of each.

Many employed investors are familiar with the 401(k) [RRSP in Canada] which creates a tax deduction up front in return for taxable income once money is withdrawn at retirement. When employers are matching your contributions, it makes sense to take advantage of the match up to the allowable maximum set up by your employer.

The Roth IRA [TFSA in Canada] is a tax-free account in which investment capital that has already been taxed can grow and compound over time to be used tax free at a future date. "Self-directed" IRA [TFSA] accounts have many more investment choices beyond just a small selection of mutual funds, ETF's or bonds typically offered in 401(k) accounts.

Finally, an individual margin account allows you the greatest investment choice flexibility from stocks to options to commodities plays. This type of account gives you greater control over making money whether the market is heading up or everyone else is panicking in a sell-off. For example, since my TFSA account is maxed out for lifetime contributions, any future investment capital is directed into my margin account.

Factor #7: Diversification Across Investment Strategies.

It is well-documented that some investment strategies work better under certain economic conditions than others. Consistently using a few time-tested solid performers will help to boost your overall returns, which brings us to looking at some specific simple strategies for dividend investing and covered call writing.

As you can surmise, by taking into consideration these various diversification factors, you'll be in a more solid position to protect your downside while generating more consistent returns in the future. Let's take a look at the first core investment strategy.

The Dividend Investment Strategy:

Investing in top-quality dividend-paying stocks need not be a complicated selection process. Our primary objectives are to:

Goal #1: Obtain a consistent dividend payment.

The payments are usually quarterly from U.S. companies and semi-annually or annually from foreign holdings. Ideally the more frequent the payout schedules the better. You want to be able to have some control over when you receive your dividend payments. Remember that the name of the game is cash flow. If you have to wait a year to be rewarded for holding onto the stock ensure that the company is a grower over time, otherwise you may be sitting on dead money.

Look for a payout ratio of less than 60 percent. The payout ratio is the amount of the annual dividend that is paid from the most recent 12-month earnings per share, which is called the trailing 12-month EPS. The lower the payout ratio the more money that is available to the company to finance growth and service debt. The good news is that the average dividend payout ratio of the S&P 500 companies has dropped from about 53 to 42 percent since 1994. This low payout ratio is good for investors.

To keep things as simple as possible, consider using **Charles Carlson's** Big Safe Dividend's formula along with his Quadrix score to initially identify top-quality dividend payers.

A word of caution though - always do a quick check of the company's numbers by visiting any financial website reporting on the stock market. What I mean by financial numbers are the 10 key indicators discussed in the previous chapters. In doing so, you minimize your chances of selecting a business that is not appropriate for the strategies being discussed. You'll want to compare your short list of stocks to the criteria listed below in order to ensure that the stock will work effectively in an accelerated cash flow model.

Goal #2: Seek a respectable dividend yield.
As you recall the dividend yield is simply the interest rate you receive on your money. As a general rule of thumb, those yields that fall into a range of 2 to 4 percent emphasize growth of capital while those companies whose yields are between 4 and 6 percent favor providing an income stream for their shareholders. To simplify the notion of dividend yield, we'll break the range of potential yields into the above two categories - income and growth.

Although you may be tempted to look for a high dividend yield above 6 or 7 percent in order to maximize your cash flow stream, you must also factor in some crucial variables. Your investment objective is not to maximize your profits but to **optimize** your profits. What I mean by this is that you need to assess whether the dividend payout level is sustainable, tax-advantaged and allows you to layer on options strategies in order to augment your overall performance.

Many high-yielders with payout ratios in excess of 90 percent can fall on difficult times, slashing the dividend or eliminating it completely. Real estate investment trusts of REITs have such extreme payout ratios. This leaves them vulnerable. REITs also are disadvantaged in that they do not receive the preferential 15 percent U.S. tax rate afforded to other dividend-paying stocks. Recently REITs were given the option of paying out up to 90 percent of their intended dividend in the form of stock. Not all investors want to repurchase shares of stock. Should you choose to go the way of the REIT ensure that it is paying out its dividend in cash, not stock.

Master Limited Partnerships (MLPs) also fall into this same category as REITs for high payout ratios. MLPs are publicly traded partnerships that typically invest in hard assets such as real estate and commodities. They also may be set up to invest in energy-related assets such as gas pipelines and storage facilities. MLPs are more sensitive to market volatility than stocks in general. Since they heavily rely on credit to fund expansion, rising interest rates tend to drive stock prices down. During economic downturns, a lower end-user demand for energy products and commodities could lead to lower dividends. Another disadvantage of owning MLPs vs. blue chip companies is that they can create potentially complex tax issues for the investor. MLP investors are limited partners who receive K-1 statements at tax time. These can be a challenge to decipher, like some of the puzzles seen on the hit TV show Survivors.

Goal #3: Receive a reasonable dividend growth rate.
As we've already seen, the power of dividend investing comes from the compounding effect of the dividend yield plus the growth rate of that dividend plus any appreciation in the stock price.

As **Charles Carlson** so succinctly puts it "You don't need big yields to generate big dividends. In fact, in many cases the biggest dividends over time come from moderate yielders that grow their dividends regularly." If cash flow from your dividend stocks is your current priority then look for income producers with dividend growth rates in the range of 6 to 10 percent.

Goal #4: Find large enough companies trading in the options market.

Once again, we would like to be able to have the opportunity to generate cash flow from multiple sources by layering cash flow strategies on top of core positions.

Business size is an important consideration when assessing the suitability of a particular stock for an accelerated cash flow system. Ideally, you would like to find a company offering an attractive dividend that is also actively traded in the options market. The company should be large enough so that you can easily move into and out of options contracts with narrow bid-ask spreads.

The bid price is what Mr. Market would like to buy the option contract at. This is the price that you the options trader will be able to sell that particular option. When you sell, you look at the bid price to gauge what you might receive for your option premium. While the ask price is the price Mr. Market is willing to spend. This is what you would have to pay in order to buy back your contracts. This number is always higher than the bid. It costs you more to buy back contracts than to sell them and receive a premium. Large spreads make it more challenging to consistently profit from any options plays.

I like to look for businesses with a market cap of at least $250 million. You may wish to start with a higher threshold of $500 million to make your options plays easier when starting out.

Let's summarize:
We're looking for high-quality blue-chip stocks with a historical repetitive pattern of both paying out dividends and increasing the dividend payments over time. A blue-chip stock is a mature, large company whose major growth phase from a regional powerhouse to an international player are behind them. They are steady growers often offering dividends to both entice and reward shareholders for holding onto their stock. By investing in larger companies, you also increase your profit potential by being able to write covered calls on the stock that you own.

Here are the basic characteristics and suitability of income and growth producers for certain types of investors:
1. Income dividend companies.
Characteristics:
1. Payout ratio 30 to 60 percent.
2. Yields 4 to 6 percent (usually in excess of 10-year Treasuries).
3. Annual dividend growth rate 6 to 10 percent.
4. Company has a record of strong financials.
5. These are steady growers with strong immediate income potential.

What type of investor benefits most from an income approach?
- An investor nearing retirement who is looking for a high stream of cash flow.
- An accelerated cash flow investor, no matter what the age.

2. Growth dividend companies.

Characteristics:
1. Payout ratio < 30 percent - companies choose to invest in future growth.
2. Low yields of 2 to 4 percent.
3. High growth rate for dividends in excess of 10 percent.
4. Strong company financials with an emphasis on profitability. Earnings per share and sales growth rates will be high coupled with a low debt load.
5. These growth companies provide solid capital appreciation in the stock price coupled with income gains over time.

What type of investor benefits most from a growth approach?
- A young investor with many years ahead and who has yet to reach their peak earning potential. With a long-term investment horizon youngsters can focus on aggressive growth via capital appreciation vs. cash flow.
- A middle-aged investor in ones' peak earning years who forgoes current income generation in favor of building capital. This might occur when one is building up enough capital for a college tuition or real estate down payment.

Who knows, you may want to dabble in the rental real estate market after learning how to create wealth in the stock market. It's something to consider down the road, right?

How to buy dividend-paying stocks:

When buying dividend-paying stocks a number of dates will be announced by the company. You'll hear the terms ex-date and record date. The record date is the date that the dividend appears in your brokerage account. The ex or ex-dividend date occurs two days before the record date. If you buy a dividend stock on or after the ex-date you do not collect the dividend.

As *Jim Cramer* says in his book *Getting Back to Even* you must focus on "the must-own date, the last day when you have to buy the stock to be able to claim its next dividend payout. The must-own date is the day before the ex-date." In a nutshell: ensure that you own the stock at least 3 days prior to the record date in order to capture the dividend.

We'll take a look at a few entry and exit strategies in the next chapter when we look at the 4th aspect of the FAST formula - Timing.

Top 10 Dividend Stock Investment Tips:

Here are my top 10 tips for investing in dividend-paying stocks:

Tip #1: In order to receive the preferred 15 percent U.S. tax rate on dividends you must hold your dividend stock a minimum of 61 days within the 121-day period surrounding the ex-dividend date. The period begins 60 days before the ex-dividend date. The bottom line is that you should avoid trading your dividend stocks frequently during the course of the year if you would like to capture the 15 percent preferred tax rate.

Tip #2: Avoid using any dividend capture strategies that try to exploit a weakness in the minimum holding period. Commissions, taxes and the natural slight downward price movement of the stock at the record date to adjust for the dividend payment are not worth the effort.

Yes, there is a slight downward price adjustment that occurs to the stock price at the record date to account for capital being taken out of the business and no longer available for growth or debt obligations. In most cases, the downward adjustment is hardly noticeable during the course of the normal trading for the week.

Tip #3: Pay attention to the following red flags that the dividend yield may be too high:

1. If the yield is 3 percent or more than the yield of typical stocks in its sector. The Value Line Investment Survey found in many libraries has average yields for sectors or you can check out other sources online for the same information.
2. If the yield is more than 4 times the overall market yield for the Dow Jones Industrial Average or the S&P 500. Barron's Market Laboratory section has the weekly market averages. Once again check with your local library to see if they carry the magazine.
3. If the yield is more than twice its historical long-run average yield. Value Line is a good source of current info.

Why pay attention to high yields? Usually, extraordinary high yields don't result from the company increasing its dividends. It's usually the result of falling stock prices due to a systemic problem.

Tip #4: Avoid using the Dividend Reinvestment Program feature offered by most dividend providers for the reinvestment of your dividend payments where additional partial and full shares of stock are automatically purchased on your behalf.

You're better off accumulating cash in your account and then allocating your capital for the best opportunity on hand. This way you can take advantage of mispricing in the market, as well as have the flexibility to move into and out of positions easier. For example, should you be selling covered calls on your dividend stock and it is called away, which is another way of saying sold at your agreed upon rental price, then you'll be left with a handful of full and partial shares to deal with. Don't worry, we'll take a look at this scenario later in this chapter and the next.

You could always buy back into the same stock; however, a better opportunity may present itself at that particular moment. You're always better off taking direct control over your cash and deciding *how* and *when* to invest it.

Tip #5: Avoid dollar cost averaging. Dollar cost averaging is the automatic allocation of investment capital to purchase stock at specific time intervals. The theory behind dollar cost averaging is that by investing on a monthly basis you reduce your overall risk of getting into the market with a lump sum of money on a bad day when the stocks are overvalued only to see the stock price drop the next day. Unfortunately, your stock broker will probably benefit the most from this approach since the recurring transaction fees on the small trades being placed boosts your broker's bottom line, not yours.

Studies have shown that during bull markets, where stock prices are rising, dollar cost averaging actually decreases your returns. Over time stocks increase in value to higher and higher prices. The simple proof can be seen by looking at a 20 or 30-year graph of the S&P 500 Index. With dollar cost averaging you're systematically paying more for your stock since the vast majority of stocks appreciate over time.

The simple solution is to purchase your stock in blocks when the stock is experiencing a slight pullback in price or the market is going through a slight correction. By buying on these slight dips you build in a margin of safety into your stock purchases.

The lower transaction costs of periodic purchases plus the satisfaction that you know you are in control of how and when to allocate your capital is a winning formula. How much better would that be? Would that increase your chances of building your wealth?

Tip #6: Your primary objective with any position that you undertake, is to optimize not maximize your returns. With dividend-paying stocks there is a tendency of inexperienced investors to seek out high yields thinking that that is the way to cash flow riches.

What you're ultimately trying to achieve is a balance between an appropriate level of yield, dividend growth and the ability to write covered calls on the stock in order to generate consistent safe returns.

This should be your primary focus for any transaction. Don't let greed blind you to what really matters the most - the ability to preserve and grow your capital. Do you follow me so far?

Tip #7: Once again the name of the game in today's investing environment is the velocity of your money. Avoid falling in love with a particular stock or brand and stubbornly hold onto it while it begins to experience a major price decline due to changing fundamentals. There is a tendency to get too emotionally attached to particular holdings that we hold dear to our hearts for whatever reason.

Try to use a little more reason in assessing whether a particular holding is still meeting your overall expectations. When you treat each of your holdings as if you're simply making a business transaction that moves you closer to your dreams, then you'll be better positioned to quickly take advantage of opportunities.

You may also find that friends, family members, work colleagues or well-intentioned professionals question your moving into and out of positions during the course of a year. In all probability, they do not have the same level of financial education that you're receiving today. It's best to be patient with them knowing that they may not have had the same exposure to wealth creation systems that you do. Over time they may come to see the benefits of becoming an actively-engaged cash flow investor. In the meantime, continue to accelerate your wealth following the system.

Tip #8: Only consider swapping your dividend stocks when a new candidate offers a materially higher prospective overall return than the least attractive dividend stock you already own. Look at your new opportunity based on the following simple criteria:
(i) Can I generate at least a percentage point higher in my overall return than my least-attractive holding?
(ii) Is this new prospect capable of meeting my minimum expectations of any stock in my portfolio? If not, wait until a better opportunity presents itself.

When trading up dividend stocks you can do so based on a better yield being offered or on a better rate of dividend growth. Ideally, seek out both.

In reality, moving into and out of dividend stock positions happens infrequently over the course of a year. This is because of your primary objective of being able to capture the dividend for cash flow. Having said this, you'll naturally hold onto positions for at least two or three months enabling you to create some magic with both the dividend payment and potential covered call on your core position. If your core positions are consistently growing over time and nothing has changed to signal that the dividends are no longer safe, keep milking your cash cows for as long as possible. Moooving along.

Tip #9: Whenever possible, try to purchase a total of 400 or 500 shares in round lots of 100 so that you can also layer in options plays for additional cash flow. When you sell 4 or 5 covered call option contracts (where 1 option contract is equal to 100 shares of stock) at a time you reduce the effects of commissions decreasing your net premium. Keep in mind that the fewer the contracts being sold, the more commissions will begin to erode your premium profits.

Tip #10: *Charles Carlson* offers this word of advice: "When possible shield your income-producing and high-turnover investments in IRAs [TFSA in Canada] and place your low-turnover or low-yielding investments in taxable accounts." Ideally, we would like to protect our compounding cash flow within a tax-favored or tax-exempt account, especially when selling covered calls on our dividend-paying stocks. However, dividend stocks are the natural choice for a simple margin account that does not provide any tax advantages since the turnover rate is typically low and dividends are currently taxed at a favorable rate.

Four Effective Covered Call Strategies:
Now it's time to take a look at how we can integrate covered call strategies into our overall cash flow plan. Unlike you, most stock investors are limited to making money only when the stock goes up in price.

Whether you're investing for the long-haul or trading stocks every few months as opportunities present themselves, the average investor can only realistically expect a historical market return of around 10% or slightly higher should they be adept at moving into and out of the market.

In real estate, an investor can buy a piece of property in the hopes that the property will increase in price over time. The concept is no different from the stock investor buying a particular stock in the hopes that it too will go up in price. The real estate investor can create a monthly cash flow by renting out his investment. In exchange for a roof over one's head, the real estate investor is paid a monthly rent.

The stock investor can also rent out his stock in the form of covered call options. However, there's no roof over one's head in this situation. The stock investor can receive cash up front in exchange for the right of the buyer who put up the cash to buy the stock should it reach an agreed upon price.

When you become a covered call writer, someone who rents out their stock in exchange for a monthly or bi-monthly rental premium, your ability to generate additional profits under varying market conditions increases. You can make money when the stock goes up to your agreed upon rental price or what is known as the strike price. This occurs most often in an upward trending or bullish market. You'll often capture both the rental premium and any stock price appreciation between your initial price and the strike price.

You can make money when the stock goes nowhere by capturing the rental premium. This occurs when the markets or the stock are neutral or flat over a period of time.

You can also protect your money better should the stock experience a slight drop in price over the course of a month or so. When a stock or the market is bearish and trending lower covered calls offer some downside protection of your stock price. This is accomplished by having your rental premium lowering your initial cost basis for the stock, thus providing a slight cushion against loss of capital.

As you can see, the selling of covered calls, increases your ability to generate additional cash flow from your investments. Under normal market conditions, a covered call writer can expect a monthly return in the range of 2 to 4% in additional to any stock price appreciation. Given that you could realistically expect to sell monthly calls almost every month that equates to annual potential returns in excess of 20 to 30%. Wouldn't you like to get your hands on that little puppy?

The challenge now becomes in learning a few strategies that allow you to consistently capture those gains. When you just buy and sell stocks, the time commitment is usually minimal. You may spend a lot of time initially picking your stocks, but once you purchase those shares there is usually a minimal amount of ongoing weekly monitoring.

On the other hand, selling covered calls on your stock holdings requires another layer of monitoring above and beyond the time required for stock selection. You'll need to watch your positions on a daily basis. However, you'll only be spending a few minutes on each position to monitor the stock price in relation to the option price.

You'll also need to spend a little bit of time planning and preparing your exit and entry strategies on a monthly basis. This small investment in time each week and at the end of each month is well worth the massive increase in cash flow you could experience by being actively engaged in making money in the markets.

What would you prefer doing: slave away 30- 40 hours per week at your current job or spend a few hours of your time each week investing in a streamlined cash flow system? Makes you realize that wealth creation and being time rich can co-exist, doesn't it? A case in point, while building up my investment portfolio, my average monthly income almost equaled what I was earning working 30 hours per week.

The purpose of the following section is to do just that - provide you with four simple covered call strategies that you can use to accelerate your cash flow from stock investing. But, before we get into the nitty gritty of selling covered calls, let's take a look at a few concepts that you should be familiar with in order to better understand how you can use each of these strategies.

Options Basics:

When you sell any option contract, besides selecting the specific stock, there will be four conditions that you will need to fill in before your order is fulfilled. These four requirements are:

Condition #1: The strike price.

This is the price that you agree to sell your stock at should the price of the stock reach this specific price at any time before the contract expires. In theory, your shares of stock could be sold at any time the stock price is at or higher than your agreed upon strike price. However, the majority of the time, the sale of your shares, what is called assignment or exercising your shares, happens on the last day of the contract known as expiration Friday. Expiration Friday is always the 3rd Friday of the expiration month.

The strike price that you select can be above, at or below the current price of the stock. When the strike price is above the current price, it is known as an *out-of-the-money* call or OTM. When the strike price is at the current price, it is known as an *at-the-money* call or ATM. When the strike price is below the current price, it is known as an *in-of-the-money* call or ITM.

Condition #2: The contract expiration date.

Each options contract has a limited life expectancy that is stipulated as the contract expiration date. For a seller of options contracts (that's you) this is an advantage especially when the contract period is short as in a 1-month time frame. The most successful and consistent covered call writers like to work with monthly contracts.

As time passes there is a natural erosion of the value of an options contract, which eventually falls to zero at the end of the trading day on expiration Friday.

Condition #3: The number of contracts.
Option contracts are sold in whole number lots, where each contract controls 100 shares of stock. No fractional units or shares of stock are allowed. For example, if you have 455 shares of Apple stock, the maximum number of covered call contracts that you can sell is 4. You're unable to write a contract for the remaining 55 shares. This is why I make a strong case for trying to purchase stock in round lots of 100 shares so that you can optimize your option positions.

Condition #4: The premium price.
The total premium that you receive as a call seller is composed of two parts - value that is associated with time and intrinsic value.

To better illustrate this concept, let's take a look at a few simplified call-selling scenarios.

If you were to sell an at-the-money (ATM) call option contract for $2 with a strike price of $45 when the current stock price is hovering around $45, your premium paid would be made up of $2 of time value. This time value is based on the appreciation potential of the option. This appreciation potential takes into consideration both the time left until contract expiration and the volatility of the stock as it trades.

Here's a 2nd scenario. Should you have settled for a strike price of $46, which is above the current stock price, in other words we sold an out-of-the-money (OTM) call for $1; it would be made up only of time value, nothing else. Your total premium paid to you would be made up of only the potential for option appreciation by a specified date. And this premium would get smaller the further out-of-the-money you sell your option contract for.

Now let's assume in our 3rd scenario that you purchase an in-the-money (ITM) call with a strike of $43 when the stock price is $45, and you receive a premium of $4. Notice that the option contract is now worth $2 more, having increased in value from $2 to $4, when we looked at our initial ATM call. This second part that makes up the total premium is attributed to intrinsic value. Intrinsic value just tells you if the option has any true or real value. It's related to how much a particular option is in-the-money giving us some actual tangible value. In this case, the call option is now $2 in-the-money.

Another way of looking at intrinsic value is that the further in-the-money the option is the greater it's intrinsic value. This value is approximately equal to the number of dollars that the stock price is in-the-money.

Yes, I realize that this is an over-simplification of the premium calculation process. My intent is to illustrate the relationship between time and intrinsic value. In the real world, the time value component would probably have adjusted downwards slightly due to the effects of time erosion on the option contract.

To recap, the four basic parameters that you will need to initially input after selecting your specific stock when you sell a covered call contract are:
1. Strike price.
2. Expiration date.
3. Number of contracts.

4. Premium price.

When you're in your online discount brokerage account, you're best served by placing a "limit" order that is good for the day for your option order rather than sending the order in as a "market" order. By placing a limit price for your orders, you have greater control over the price you could end up initially selling your contracts at and also the price you're willing to buy them back at, if necessary, as part of your exit strategy. We'll look at this and other timing strategies in greater detail for entering and exiting the market in the following chapter.

Now that we have an idea as to which parameters we need to enter for each call option position that we undertake, let's take a look at four simple call selling strategies to place in your investment arsenal. Please keep in mind that these strategies are not carved in stone. As with any strategy, they are to be used as a guideline in helping you make the best investment choices that'll accelerate your cash flow and provide some protection of your capital.

Since markets trend upwards over time, let's take an initial look at how you can tap into stocks that are showing some price appreciation.

Option Strategy #1: Growth Generation in Up-Trending Markets.
A growth strategy for call options is one that allows for both gains to be made in the stock price appreciation, as well as premium received from selling your calls.

This strategy works best under the following four conditions:
Condition #1: The stock and the market as a whole are experiencing an upward bullish trend with low volatility.

We want investors to be confident enough in the global economy to invest their capital in growing businesses in the global markets. This information can be seen on a technical chart of both a broad-based index such as the S&P 500 and the stock being analyzed. Take a look at the stock's price and trading volume over several months of graphed data points. I like to use the free charting tools found at StockCharts.com.

From the technical chart of the S&P 500 Index the overall market should be appreciating over the time frame selected. Being visual in nature the graphic representation of the historical data is easier for you to identify patterns that have unfolded in a particular stock.

Condition #2: The second condition to assess is if the 200-day and 50-day simple moving-day averages are moving in a positive direction on high volume. The moving day average is a popular technical indicator that shows the value of a stock over a specific time period. Traders who use trend-following strategies are drawn to what moving averages can tell them about the direction the stock's price may be headed. Look for the moving-day averages of the market to be trending higher.

The other part to the equation is to see if the market and the stock are trading on above average volume. High volume equates to confidence in the stock and the underlying business. Trading volume will tell you whether or not investors are putting their money on the line.

Condition #3: The third aspect to quickly assess is whether or not the positive momentum of the stock price is continuous and not a spike. Ideally, we are looking for price appreciation that is occurring gradually over that 3 to 6-month window.

Two other technical indicators to consider using in conjunction with moving-day averages are the MACD and the Relative Strength Index or RSI. Here's a simple description of each technical indicator:

(a) MACD

The MACD or Moving Average Convergence Divergence is a popular momentum indicator that helps determine when a trend has ended or begun and may reverse direction.

This technical indicator uses two moving average lines and a zero line. The solid black line is called the MACD line and the slower moving red or dotted line is the signal line. When the MACD line crosses above the signal line and the zero line this indicates a positive trend in the market. I prefer looking at a histogram representation of the indicator to graphically tell me when a trend is reversing. The default setting for the MACD is 12, 26, 9. I like to use a more sensitive setting of 8, 17, 9. You may wish to do the same.

(b) RSI

The other popular indictor is the relative strength index or RSI which helps to determine if an individual stock has been oversold or overbought by investors. I touched on this indicator in the chapter on how to assess the growth potential of various businesses.

The RSI is an oscillator that moves between 0 and 100. When the RSI rises above 70 or 80, it's a signal that the stock is overbought and money may begin to flow out of the security causing a price decline. On the flip side, when the RSI falls below 30 or 20, it's a signal that the stock is oversold and investors may begin to buy the security causing the stock price to rise.

This particular indicator works best with individual stocks, as opposed to the market as a whole, and with a short-term time frame such as a few weeks. It's therefore a useful tool for the call option seller or buyer. Stocks with a rising RSI above 50 and below 80, fall into our sweet spot for potential growth candidates.

We'll take a more in-depth look at how to use technical indicators when we delve into entry and exit strategies for all of our stock and option positions.

Condition #4: The stock is in a strong industry. Sectors and industries tend to go in and out of favor with institutional buyers and retail investors as a whole. Often the popularity of a specific industry or sector is heavily influenced by current economic trends in the global marketplace. For example, tech stocks were all the craze in 2012 with the massive popularity of the mobile internet. Stocks that are in favor with Mr. Market have an easier time of seeing appreciating stock prices.

Growth Generation Strategy Advantages.
There are three major advantages of using the growth generation strategy, namely:
1. You profit from both the option premium received and the upside appreciation of the stock.
2. You have less of a chance of your stock being assigned and called away (i.e. cashed out) at the end of the option cycle since the stock price has further to rise than an at-the-money call option strategy.
3. Time decay works in your favor since there is no intrinsic value, only time value. As time lapses, the option premium approaches zero, accelerating even faster just days prior to expiration Friday.

Growth Generation Strategy Disadvantages.
The top three disadvantages are that:
1. You have the least amount of downside protection should the stock decline in value, since there is no intrinsic value had you bought an in-the-money call.
2. You'll probably receive an initial premium that is low. The further away the strike price is from the current stock price the lower the premiums. An at-the-money call yields you the highest "initial" premiums.
3. You'll probably pay more to close your position should the stock price drop. This is due to the relationship between stock price and option price known as Delta.

The term Delta, or hedge ratio, is defined as the amount an option price will change given a 1-point change in the price of the stock. It tells you the relationship between a stock's price movement and the option's price movement.

Delta values range from 0 to 1 for call options. For example, if the stock moves up 3 points and the option delta is equal to 1 or 100%, the option will also move up 3 points.

This particular relationship often exists with in-the-money calls where an increase in the stock price is almost equal dollar for dollar with an increase in the option price. As a rule of thumb, a stock that is at-the-money, meaning that its price is at or near the option's strike price will have a delta of approximately 0.5 on the zero to 1 scale.

As the stock's price drops the delta approaches zero. There is less movement in the price of the option in relation to the stock price the further it drops.

What does all this mean? The delta provides you with a means to compare the interaction between the stock and option pricing for a particular stock.

When using a growth strategy, keep in mind that it will probably be more expensive to close your option position as the stock price declines, which may limit your profitability on the contract. What's important to know is that option's pricing is dynamic since the erosion of time has an impact on pricing especially as one approaches expiration and all options contracts fall to zero.

Okay, okay ... I know that I may have overwhelmed you with that whole thing about Delta. When your head stops spinning like a whirling dervish, take a deep breath before reading on.

Here's an example of how you might structure a growth play.

Example #1: Growth Generation in a Bull Market.
Let's say you're looking at a technical chart of the stock Medifast, symbol MED. And over the past couple of months the stock has been showing positive growth signs as evidenced by the upward movement of the stock price with both the 200-day and 50-day moving averages.

You decide to investigate further and notice that Medifast has had above average volume. It has a relative strength index that is above 50 and below 80. As well, you notice that the MACD indicator is above the horizontal zero line indicating that momentum in the stock is positive.

You determine that you have a number of positive signals that allow you to better execute a growth strategy. Now you need to take a look at the various option prices and select an appropriate strike price that'll hopefully give you a monthly return of 2 to 4% - our sweet spot.

So, What's the Profit Potential?
A simple way to determine which strike price meets your objectives is to just plug in four key parameters into the Ellman spreadsheet (see The Blue Collar Investor) or create a similar one yourself.

To assess the profitability of various strike prices, log into your broker's website that lists the various call option strike prices. You'll need to enter:

1. The strike price of the two options just "above" the current price of the stock.
2. The dollar value of the two option premiums.
3. The price you paid for the stock initially and the number of shares purchased. Remember we ideally want round lots of 100 so that we can sell one option contract per 100 shares of stock owned.
4. The number of option contracts you would like to sell (ideally 4 -5 contracts so as to minimize the effects of transaction fees).

Let's assume that the initial stock price was $33.00 in mid-March and that there were two strike prices just above the stock price.

The lower strike price of $34 was going to give you a premium of $1.00 from the sale producing an immediate option return of 3.0%, while a higher strike of $36 gives you $0.50 for an option return of 1.5%.

These dollar values would be immediately deposited into your account should a buyer take you up on the offer to purchase the contracts at the agreed upon premium. You actually won't have to worry about finding a specific buyer, Mr. Market sets this up seamlessly behind the scenes. In essence, you would receive $100 for every option contract sold at a strike of 34 and $50 for every option contract sold at the higher strike of 36. Recall that you control 100 shares of stock therefore the premium listed is multiplied by a factor of 100 in order to arrive at the actual amount of premium deposited directly into your brokerage account.

Your maximum potential total return based on the option premium received plus the maximum stock appreciation that you could realize gives you a potential of 6.0% for the lower strike price of 34 and 10.6% for the higher strike of 36.

Please keep in mind that these are hypothetical returns based on the premise that your stock will appreciate in value up to the strike price and be called away (sold at the strike price).

Your decision as to which opportunity is going to get you closer to your objectives should place a greater weight on how much of a premium you could receive up front vs. what the potential might be if the stock appreciates in price.

As a rule of thumb, select a higher strike price for stocks that you plan on holding for more than one month. For example, a higher strike price makes sense if you have a dividend-paying stock from which you would like to generate some additional monthly cash flow. If you're not partial to the stock, then selecting a lower strike price with a richer up-front premium may make more sense for your cash flowing investments.

After you've assessed the cash flow potential for each scenario using your spreadsheet, you'll need to decide on the specific strike price and the associated option premium that's best for you.

When you actually place your sell-to-open order on your online brokerage trading platform, you'll be placing a limit order between the bid and ask prices for the option, rather than a market order. The limit price provides greater control over the actual price you'll receive in option premiums.

Let's move on to the next option strategy that of income generation in primarily neutral markets.

Option Strategy #2: Income Generation in Neutral Markets.

An income strategy for call options is one that attempts to capture high premiums from your call selling. This strategy works best under the following three conditions:

Condition #1: The stock and the market as a whole are trading sideways or flat with little or no price appreciation on average volume.

Condition #2: The 200-day and 50-day simple moving-day averages are leveling out and may be converging.

Condition #3: The technical indicators such as MACD and RSI are not giving any clear buy or sell signals.

Income Generation Strategy Advantages.

There are two major advantages of using the income generation strategy, namely:

1. It provides the highest initial option return resulting in a pure income generation play.
2. It takes advantage of maximizing immediate cash flow into your brokerage account.

Income Generation Strategy Disadvantages.

The top three disadvantages are that:
1. You have no upside potential for stock price appreciation.
2. There is also no downside protection as with an in-the-money call position.
3. You have a high probability of stock being called away (sold).

Example #2: Income Strategy in a Flat Market.

Let's assume that Medifast is trading with a stock price of $44.10 as of mid-June. And when you look at a technical chart of the stock, you see that this stock has been trading sideways. You also notice that for the past 2 months trading volume has been average.

The 50-day moving average is virtually flattening out and both the 200-day and 50-day moving averages are converging (moving closer to each other). You also observe that the relative strength index is hovering around 50 giving no clear buy or sell signals. And the same holds for the MACD indicator.

With an income generation strategy, your goal is to capture the highest call option premium possible knowing that in all likelihood your stock will be called away on or before expiration Friday and that your potential profit will be derived solely from the call premium.

After you have logged into your broker's website that lists the various call option strike prices you'll need to enter the following information into your spreadsheet or Ellman Option Calculator:
- The strike price of the "closest" one or two options to the current price of the stock
- The dollar value of the one or two option premiums

- The price you paid for the stock initially and the number of shares purchased. Once again, we want round lots of 100 so that we can sell one option contract per 100 shares of stock owned.
- The number of option contracts you would like to sell.

Let's assume a strike price of 44 gives you $1.30 from the sale producing an immediate return of 2.9%. Each option contract sold would generate $130 which would be immediately deposited into your account.

This percentage represents the maximum expected return on your investment. You do not participate in any upside growth potential of the stock price appreciating. However, you can capitalize on the maximum premium value associated with the calls since they are at-the-money.

If on expiration Friday, July 15 the stock traded above $44 your option contracts would have been exercised and the shares sold at $44. You would have made a 1-month return of ~2.9% and are now free to enter into another profitable opportunity.

Since you've just covered a lot of material and many new concepts, it might be a good idea to take a break and resume the last section of this chapter when you're fresh. And should you find some of the concepts covered difficult to grasp at this point in time - after you have cleared your head - go back and review those specific sections.

Option Strategy #3: Protection Strategy in Down-Trending Markets.

A protection strategy for call options is one that attempts to capture premiums from your call selling as well as cushion your cash basis in your stock should the stock price decline slightly over the course of the month. This strategy works best under the following four conditions:

Condition #1: The stock and the market as a whole are experiencing a slightly bearish and volatile market tone.

Condition #2: The 50-day simple moving-day average has crossed under the 200-day moving average moving in a negative direction.

Condition #3: Mixed technical indicators for that equity.

Condition #4: Also works well in an up-trending chart pattern but in a volatile manner.

Protection Strategy Advantages

There are three major advantages of using the protection strategy, namely:
1. You receive immediate option profit from the sale of the call.
2. The position creates downside protection for your stock price.
3. This is a lower risk strategy compared to the other call option strategies.

Protection Strategy Disadvantages

The top three disadvantages are that:
1. You have no upside potential.
2. There are lost opportunity costs since you do not participate in any potential for share appreciation.
3. You have a high probability of the stock being called away on or before expiration Friday.

Option Example #3: Protection Strategy in a Declining Market.

Let's assume that you purchased Medifast in early January at a stock price of $50. The stock was experiencing a slightly bearish trend as evidenced by the 50-day simple moving-day average crossing under the 200-day moving average moving in a negative direction. Both the MACD and relative strength index were showing short-term mixed signals. And the relative strength index had been floating above and below 50. As well, the MACD momentum indicator had been moving above and below the zero line every couple of weeks.

If you're going to take a somewhat bearish outlook on this particular stock, you would want to look at strike prices that are below the current price of the stock. Your objective is to build in some downside protection for the price of the stock to decline slightly during the course of the month.

Once again, the next step is to log into your broker's website and look at the various call option strike prices for the current month. You'll need to enter onto your spreadsheet the following information:

- The strike price of the closest two options just "below" the current price of the stock. Ideally, you're looking for strike prices with high delta values above 90%.
- The dollar value of the two option premiums.
- The price you paid for the stock initially and the number of shares purchased.
- The number of option contracts you would like to sell.

Let's say that from these two scenarios the lowest strike price of 45 gives you $5.10 from the option sale producing an immediate cash deposit of 10.2%, while the higher strike of 47.50 gives you a cash premium of $2.80 for an immediate cash deposit of 5.6%.

The other calculation that is generated from the Ellman calculator spreadsheet is the downside protection afforded by this strategy. In the first case, the lowest selected strike price of 45 reduces your cost basis for the stock from $50 to $44.90. In order for this position to lose money the stock price would have to drop below this level.

The downside protection that this deep in-the-money call has to offer is the difference between your original stock price of $50 and new cost basis price of the stock which is 10.2% lower. In other words, the stock could drop from $50 to $44.90 or 10.2% before you would be negatively impacted by the falling price.

The second higher strike price of 47.50 reduces your cost basis of the stock from $50 to $47.20 which gives you 5.6% of downside protection.

Both strikes have some time value that you can profit from should the stock remain above the strike price of the call options all the way to expiration.

With the lower strike of 45 you have 10 cents of time value premium (i.e. $45.00 - $44.90) that you can capture should the stock be exercised and called away. The 10 cents would give you a 0.2% monthly return. Not much in the way of income, however you're using this particular strategy for the downside protection that it offers in a slightly down trending market and not for income generation.

You may find that periodically using this strategy for your dividend paying stocks affords you some protection, as well as potentially capturing a dividend payment.

On the flip side, the higher strike of 47.50 has 30 cents of time value giving you a potential monthly return of 0.6%. The intrinsic value for this particular strike was calculated by subtracting the 47.50 strike price from the current stock price of 50 giving you 2.50. And the time value is the difference between the 2.50 in intrinsic value and the total premium of 2.80 leaving you with the 30 cents.

Your decision now becomes, how much protection you need vs. immediate cash generated. Realize that this strategy works best with declining stock prices that are temporary in nature. The market will eventually trend higher. Using this strategy in an upward trending market will in all likelihood produce losses.

Now that we have gone through the three basic strategies for selling covered calls, let's take a look at how we can use one particular covered call strategy to generate not only a better dividend yield on stock that we're holding onto for more than a few months but a significant potential return from both the call premium and dividend payments.

Option Strategy #4: Increasing Dividend Yield Strategy.
One conservative way to increase your dividend yield is to sell a long-term in-the-money call. This strategy works best under the following four conditions:
Condition #1: The stock and the market as a whole are trading sideways or flat with little or no price appreciation on average volume.

Condition #2: You would like to hold onto the stock for the dividend payments and possibly as a replacement strategy for the conservative portion of your portfolio which is typically bonds.

Condition #3: The current dividend yield falls into the 3 to 6% range.

Condition #4: The stock must offer longer-term options contracts which have expiration dates greater than 8 or 9 months out.

Dividend Yield Strategy Advantages.

There are five major advantages of using the increased dividend yield strategy, namely:

1. You receive an option premium that creates significant downside protection.
2. The premium received decreases your cost basis for your stock which significantly increases your dividend yield.
3. You receive immediate cash from the call option which can be used elsewhere plus your quarterly dividends.
4. This strategy requires less time to monitor your position than monthly option plays.
5. It's easy to determine your maximum profit and breakeven point on the stock.

Dividend Yield Strategy Disadvantages.

The top three disadvantages are that:

1. You'll receive lower returns than selling 1-month call options.
2. You have no upside potential since you have an obligation to sell at the strike price.
3. You risk assignment, the stock being called away, at any time and you'll likely be assigned by expiration Friday unless you use an exit strategy. More on this in the next chapter.

Option Example #4: Dividend Yield Strategy.

Let's say that you purchased a dividend-paying stock like Freeport McMoran Copper & Gold, in late May for $31.25 with a projected yield of 4%. And that you purchased 400 shares of this stock so that you could write (sell) a long-term call option in order to increase your overall return.

The first order of business would be to select a couple of option strike prices for comparison that are at least one option contract "below" the current stock price. As well, you're looking for an expiration date that is more than 6 months out in order to capture at least two quarterly dividend payments.

After doing some initial research, you select two possible candidates to assess: a January 2019 contract with a 31 strike price paying a premium of $5.05 per option contract and the other with a 29.50 strike price and premium of $5.95.

This particular option date allows you the potential to capture up to 3 dividend payments based on the historical dividend payouts that typically occur in mid-July, October and January.

Once you plug these values into your spreadsheet you would be able to see that the 31 strike gives you a potential effective dividend yield of 4.7%. This is calculated by dividing the current annual dividend by the original price of the stock less the premium we receive. In effect, the premium reduces your cost basis in the stock which increases your effective yield on the dividend.

The lower strike of 29.50 gives you an effective yield of 4.9%. Not bad a bad interest rate in today's markets. And your immediate option return with a 31 strike produces 16.2%.

Recall that you purchased 400 shares of Freeport McMoran. This gives you $505 per option contract or $2050 deposited into your brokerage account. The potential 7-month total return which includes capturing 3 dividend payouts is 18.4% or $2425, which is great on an initial investment of $12,500. Can you see the income generation potential from this particular strategy?

It should become more evident that a little investment knowledge can accelerate your cash flow potential and help you realize your dreams that much faster. Periodically selling covered calls on solid dividend-paying companies is one such vehicle.

But that's not all, for the lower strike your immediate option return is 19% giving you $2380. And this cash is deposited up front into your brokerage account. Could you reinvest a portion of the proceeds into another cash-flowing opportunity accelerating the velocity of your money? Of course you could. Your potential 7-month total return is 20.4% or $2755 on an initial investment of $12,500.

Once again, your choice becomes a personal one as to which strike to accept based on your current assessment of the market, future expectations for your stock and your comfort level. Key to this strategy is that you'll need to plan an exit strategy that allows you to optimize your profitability on the holding. We'll take a look at worst case - best case scenarios in the next chapter that gets into several timing strategies.

There you have it four great covered call option strategies that'll accelerate your cash flow. I would strongly recommend exploring some of the covered call writing scenarios posted on various You Tube channels like The Blue Collar Investor. A visual walk-through helps you pick up the concepts that much faster.

Top 15 Covered Call Strategy Tips:
To wrap up this section on selling calls, here are my top 15 strategy tips for writing covered calls on stock that you own. Even

though, you've seen some of these key concepts before, they're worth repeating and re-stating with a slightly different perspective.

Tip #1: Learn before you earn.

Don't invest in anything you do not understand. No matter what your investment strategy, take the time to learn the basics so that you can make appropriate investment decisions. I encourage you to tap into the wealth of knowledge being shared by some of the educators mentioned in this book. Check out your appendix for resources to explore down the road.

Tip #2: Keep your options investment system simple.

Keep your technical analysis as simple and easy as possible. I only use a handful of technical indicators to guide my decision-making. Also, avoid using time intensive systems. If you are having to personally track and update a myriad of multiple variables on a daily basis, start looking for an easier approach. Life is too short to be pre-occupied with your investments day in and day out. Wouldn't you agree?

Tip #3: Spread out your capital.

Don't put all of your eggs in one basket. You should have no more than 20% of your investment capital in any one industry and preferably spread across the 11 economic sectors. Industries can go out of favor very quickly. You should also spread out your capital across investment strategies to optimize your portfolio for consistent profitability.

Having a rigid money-management system in place allows me to both preserve my capital and maintain a high level of confidence in my abilities. I plan to be in the options trading business for years to come; therefore, I know that there will be hundreds of profitable positions that I'll be able to participate in over time. No need to rush the journey and risk my hard-earned dollars.

Tip #4: Use an online discount broker where ever possible.

Full service brokerage fees will quickly erode your returns on your investments. If you trade options several times per month the high transaction costs of a full-service broker will also negatively impact your trading decisions by having you hold onto positions longer than you should because you don't want to incur the big fees.

Tip #5: Always pick stocks for options trading that are fundamentally sound.

Whether you use the selection criteria outlined in this guide or criteria from a reputable source, always seek the best of breed businesses within a specific industry. You can make a lot more money with options plays by choosing companies that have a proven track record for growth especially if they are market leaders.

Tip #6: Monitor your holdings on a regular basis.

This enables you to optimize your profits by using appropriate exit strategies when the time comes. You need not spend an inordinate amount of time verifying the fundamentals and looking at a technical chart of your positions. However, you do need to be positioned to take advantage of money-making opportunities as they present themselves.

Tip #7: Learn to use a variety of options strategies, not just one.

For example, don't just sell out-of-the money covered calls just because they're one of the most popular options strategies. Base your investment decisions on the direction and mood of the market, as well as what the current technicals are indicating for a particular opportunity play.

Tip #8: Watch the greed factor.

Don't sell covered calls that generate excessively high monthly returns. Your sweet spot for monthly returns should be in the range of 2 to 4%; anything higher than 5% may be a sign of higher stock volatility.

Tip #9: Avoid selling covered calls on stocks that have a quarterly earnings report during the same month.

Earnings reports can create excessive volatility whereby the stock is now trading over a much wider price range. Better to watch the stock over the month and re-evaluate its suitability after the earnings report is public.

Tip #10: Be mindful of transaction fees.

Try to sell (rent out) at least 4 or 5 contracts (1 option contract = 100 shares of stock) at a time in order to reduce the effects of commissions decreasing your net premium. The fewer the contracts being sold; the more commissions will begin to erode your premium profits.

As a general word of caution, avoid selling covered calls in rapidly rising or falling markets. These markets are rare, occurring every 4 to 6 years, so most of the time, covered call writing is an appropriate strategy.

A rapidly declining market is best handled by sidestepping out of the stock market and moving your cash into other opportunities in possibly other asset classes or by waiting patiently in a cash or cash-equivalent position for opportunities to present themselves. On the other hand, in a rapidly rising market, you may be better served through the natural appreciation of the stock price, especially if it exceeds our 2 to 4% monthly covered call expectation.

Tip #11: Always assess the business's fundamentals, technical indicators and your mental state before placing a trade.

I ensure that all of my geese are properly lined up before placing any trade. This not only builds confidence, it also creates a better edge and higher probability of coming out on top. I also never trade on a hot tip. Take the time to do your due diligence on each potential trade. It'll have a dramatic effect on your bottom line.

Tip #12: Determine both an entry point and exit point for each opportunity.

When you pre-plan your trades, you increase your probability of success. Entering a trade when you have had a chance to clearly think through possible outcomes should be your objective every time you place a trade. Getting caught up in the excitement of the market at a specific unanticipated moment could spell disaster. Thinking through rational outcomes in advance increases your chances of pulling off a winning transaction. This thinking process takes into consideration how much capital is at risk and what specific trading parameters either increase risk or mitigate it.

Tip #13: Take full responsibility for your actions.

Do not blame the weather, your neighbor's dog or Mr. Market for the outcome of a particular investment decision. Always remember that every potential investment opportunity is unique. Learn from the mistakes that you'll inevitably make, but do not dwell on the negative outcome. All investors make errors that cost them money. I know have. How else was I going to learn what works for me and doesn't?

Your goal should be to reduce the number of errors that you can control yourself over time. Re-focus your energy and time looking for the next potential opportunity. When you look at the market as being the enemy, you take yourself out of the constant flow of opportunities that present themselves. By freeing up your mind you can now focus on moving into and out of better and better opportunities.

Tip #14: Do not place a trade if you're emotionally upset, in a euphoric mood or under above average stress from your work/ home environment.

When my emotional state is out of whack with my normal operating state, I tend to make silly mistakes that cost me money in the end. By tuning into my emotional state prior to each trade, I've been able to increase my ability to consistently place winning trades, while minimizing or eliminating common trading errors completely.

Tip #15: Optimize not maximize each trade.

It is okay for me to leave money on the table. I know that opportunities present themselves every month. The key is to *patiently* wait for those situations where you have an edge and then move back into the market taking profits when they present themselves and not feel bad if you don't maximize your profit potential.

Creating Your Edge:

To become a profitable investor, strive to create your winning mindset. When you adjust your attitude about investing in such a way that you can move in and out of opportunities without the slightest bit of fear based on a system that does not allow you to become reckless, your chances of success increase dramatically.

As **Mark Douglas** points out in his book **Trading in the Zone**: "The consistency you seek is in your mind, not the markets. It's attitudes and beliefs about being wrong, losing money and the tendency to become reckless, when you're feeling good, that causes most losses - not technique or market knowledge."

This particular chapter focused on the S component of the FAST approach to cash flow investing, namely - Strategies.

Right from the get-go we took a look at how you could create a truly diversified investment portfolio by taking into consideration seven factors that would help to reduce your overall portfolio risk. Keeping these factors in mind will help increase your odds of becoming a very successful investor.

We then spent some time delving into how to invest in top quality dividend paying stocks that also allow you to not only collect a regular dividend payment but also occasional call option premiums.

Next, we explored four different covered call strategies with specific simplified examples as to how to generate additional cash flow in varying market conditions.

In the next chapter, we'll look at the T component of the FAST approach - Timing, along with a few case studies.

Chapter 8 - Timing When to Enter & Exit Positions

Focus Questions:
1. How could I optimize my timing when moving into and out of the markets?
2. What guidelines will help improve my odds of placing successful trades?
3. How do I enter a covered call position with a "sell-to-open" transaction?
4. Should I use stop loss orders to minimize my downside losses?
5. When is it an "appropriate" time to sell my stock?
6. How do I exit a covered call position with a "buy-to-close" transaction?
7. Which four times could I place a buy-to-close order?
8. What are the three different rolling strategies for exiting a covered call position?

In this particular chapter, we'll address a variety of timing strategies for both moving into stock and option positions and exiting them in order to optimize your profitability. These particular strategies work well within the framework of the accelerated cash flow investment system. We'll focus on the letter T of the FAST approach which delves into how to better time your entry into and exit out of the stock market.

Contrary to what many in the investment landscape are saying about timing the market, you can learn to be more adept at moving into and out of positions so that you increase the probability of coming out on top.

One of the most frustrating aspects of stock investing is trying to figure out when you should move into and out of positions. It can take you years to figure out what time periods you should avoid based on the documented historical trends. It can also take the average investor years to figure out how the movement of the big institutional players affects one's ability to profit from the entry and exit points in the market.

As mentioned earlier in this book, you will in all likelihood not be able to time the market tops and bottoms, thus enabling you to maximize your profits. No one has been able to consistently do this in the stock market.

However, we can take advantage of certain times of the day, week, month or year that enable us to better optimize our profits. This knowledge helps us create our "edge" thereby increasing our profitability potential in the stock market. Ready to pick up some tips?

The following are my top dozen tips to better timing the market and more importantly why.

Tip #1: Avoid buying stock or call options on a Monday.
If you decide to move into a position on Monday morning, expect higher than normal price volatility throughout the day. According to former trading floor boss **Joe Terranova** in his book **Buy High Sell Higher**:
"Whether traders love or hate their personal lives, the pros that move the market often come into the office on Mondays in a bad mood. Whatever the reason, there is always a flood of emotion coursing through the market on Mondays. Markets that are trading on emotions are not where you want to be. I make a point of never trading on Mondays."

I tend to concur with Joe. You as a cash flow investor are better served by waiting for the markets to play out during the course of the day on Mondays. They tend to be too emotionally charged after the weekend.

Tip #2: Try to trade on Wednesdays and Thursdays.
On the flip side of the coin is to ask yourself when would be the ideal time to try to better time my market plays? Mid-week tends to present better investment opportunities than either the beginning or end of the week. According to **Jeffrey Hirsch** in his book the **Stock Trader's Almanac** Wednesday's have produced the most gains since 1990.

Often on Fridays many big institutional players unload certain positions before the weekend, preferring not to hold potentially volatile stocks that may be affected by news over the weekend. This coupled with the notion that many traders take off early on Friday afternoon means that the smaller players become the temporary price movers. Watch to see that the price movement of the stock is in synch with the volume of shares being traded. A rising stock price yet decreasing volume is a signal that the current stock price trend is unsustainable over time.

Tip #3: Avoid trading first thing in the morning and during the lunch hour.
As to what time of the day may present better buy and sell opportunities, you may be best served by waiting at least an hour or so after the opening bell before getting into the market. I have made this mistake a couple of times, only to realize later in the morning that I overpaid for my positions. Another time of the day that may be problematic is midday during the lunch hour when many professional traders take their lunch. With fewer traders market volume tends to lag.

A little patience as to seeing how the day may be unfolding may save you a few bucks in the end. By waiting until the end of the day when volume is typically the heaviest, you may be in a better position to assess your timing opportunity. Remember that above average volume with rising stock prices is a signal that investors are confident in a particular stock or the market as a whole.

Tip #4: Avoid trading at the end or beginning of a quarter.

Be very attentive as to stocks that you may be holding which have been lack luster over the past quarter. Many intuitional players unload poor performers in an attempt to re-balance their overall portfolio. Keep in mind that the mutual fund industry is very competitive and that many fund managers take a short-term approach to investing in order to hang onto their client's money.

By being vigilant at the end of each quarter you can better assess the impact of buying or selling particular holdings based on what you feel the big boys may be doing. Sometimes you can get a feel for the tone of the market as a whole by watching how money is flowing into the stock market as opposed to bond market or commodities such as gold and oil.

Tip #5: Avoid trading when company earnings are announced.

The time period just leading up to and soon after an earnings report release can see volatile stock price movement. Earnings reports can signal shifts in momentum. This is especially important when you'll be selling covered calls on the stock during the same month that earnings are going to be announced.

It may be more prudent to wait out the period around the earnings report release to see how Mr. Market will handle the information rather than commit yourself to a call position. You can always take up a position once you're assured that the news will not have a negative effect on your positions.

Tip #6: Avoid trading right after any big announcement.
Certain economic events and federal government announcements
have the power to move the markets in one direction or another.
By keeping track of those major economic or government
announcements in your appointment calendar (with the markets
so to speak), you can take advantage of opportunities as they
unfold. The economic data provided can sometimes help you
better develop your edge in the markets.

A list of possible regularly scheduled events that you could keep
your eye on, are listed below. This list is by no means exhaustive.
It does provide you with a starting point from which you can further
develop your investor's edge.

1. Institute for Supply Management - ISM Manufacturing
   Index: a growing economy shows up with the Index above
   50.
2. Department of Labor - US Unemployment Report:
   measures how tight the labor market is.
3. U.S. Treasury - 10-Year T-Note Auction: tracks investor
   movement in/out of stocks.
4. Department of Commerce - Retail Sales Report: measures
   consumer spending which helps predict economic growth.
5. Consumer Price Index (CPI): measures the effects of
   inflation on the overall economy.
6. National Association of Realtors - Existing Home Sales:
   indicates housing market trends.
7. Department of Energy Inventory Data: indicates supply and
   demand for oil & gas.
8. China Purchasing Management Index (PMI): provides a
   good picture of global manufacturing health.
9. Federal Reserve - The Beige Book: summarizes economic
   conditions.

Tip #7: Be wary of the first 2 to 3 weeks of January.

Many companies have year-end earnings announcements in January, which can translate to increased stock price volatility.

The large institutional players typically have major capital allocation flows in and out of stocks during this period of time. This is especially so with the commodity-based funds. If you've identified a commodity-based stock that you would like to invest in, you may be better served waiting on the sidelines until the big boys have finished their dance with increased price volatility.

I'm guilty of making this mistake. Instead of being more patient with purchasing a particular stock, I ended up initially paying more for the investment as the stock dropped in price mid-January. I had to wait on the sidelines for a short period of time until April for the stock to appreciate up to a level that I felt comfortable selling option contracts at.

As you know, the name of the game is increasing the velocity of your money. Unfortunately, my money was parked in a position whereby I was unable to generate a monthly cash flow. Bad boy, Randall. You should to be taken out behind the wood shed for a licking.

Tip #8: Schedule any important moves after mid-April.

The stock market tends to be more prone to weakness after the mid-month tax deadline in the United States. This may be the result of individual investor money moving out of the markets in order to pay for tax obligations owing and the rebalancing of portfolios in order take advantage of certain capital losses.

For your own personal finances, you may wish to hold off any major moves that could have an impact on your current tax liabilities owing. It may be prudent to check with a financial planner or accountant prior to making any such big moves.

Tip #9: Be cautious investing in early October.
The beginning of October has often been weak for the stock market. There tends to be fewer growth plays during this particular time period. The markets typically ramp up for the Christmas season come late October or early November.

You may wish to keep closer tabs on the market by following the fall trend of the S&P 500 Index and those specific sectors you're currently interested in. More on that in a moment.

Tip #10: Be aware of sector rotations.
Some sectors and industries show strength at certain times of the year. Large institutional players tend to support certain sectors at specific times of the year.

For example, the technology sector and consumer discretionary are usually stronger in the fall and weaker in spring. This aligns well with the expected increase in consumer spending that occurs from October to January every year.

Another example is that of the oil refiners who tend to do well in the first and fourth quarters of the year as demand for heating oil increases over the winter months.

Tip #11: Always monitor the overall market 30-day volume & 200-day moving average.
Once again, you're ideally looking for a confirmation of overall strength and confidence in the markets, such as the S&P 500 Index. This shows up with above average volume and rising moving day averages.

The ideal scenario is to see the 50-day moving average above the 100-day average which is above the 200-day moving average for the market.

As well, you should check out the technical charts of the top eleven sector ETF's known as Spiders or "SPDR". Take a look at the moving day averages to see if they are flat, up, or down. This is a simple way to verify which sectors are currently in favor with Mr. Market thereby increasing your chances of making profitable trades.

You may also want to drill down deeper by taking a look at the top 3 to 5 holdings in those sectors that interest you to see if buying opportunities may be presenting themselves.

The eleven ETF SPDRs that focus on the following sectors along with some of their biggest holdings are listed below:
1. XLK - Information Technology: Apple, Microsoft, IBM
2. XLI - Industrials: General Electric, United Technologies, UPS
3. XLRE - Real Estate: American Tower, Simon Property, Crown Castle
4. XLY - Consumer Discretionary: McDonalds, Walt Disney, Amazon
5. XLB - Materials: Freeport McMoran Copper & Gold, E.I. du Pont, Dow Chemical
6. XLP - Consumer Staples: Procter & Gamble, Phillip Morris Intl., Coca-Cola
7. XLV - Health Care: Johnson & Johnson, Pfizer, Merck
8. XLU - Utilities: Exelon, Southern Co., Dominion Resources
9. XLE - Energy: Exxon Mobil, Chevron, Conoco Phillips
10. XLF - Financials: Berkshire Hathaway, JP Morgan Chase, Wells Fargo

11. XTL - Telecommunication: Lumentum Holdings, Arista Networks, CenturyLink

Tip #12: Avoid the investo-tainment hype.

This is a tough tip to follow. It is counter-intuitive to not jump on the investing bandwagon when everyone else is singing praise for a specific stock or group of stocks. While screening for great potential stock candidates your judgment can be clouded and influenced by what you see and hear in the media.

However, you're better served by following a specific decision-making process. That process should take into account analyzing a handful of key fundamentals of the business as well as the technical charts and indicators that show you when you should enter the market.

By stepping back and taking the time to process the basic data that really matters in executing your specific investment strategy, you'll save yourself a lot of grief and heartache knowing that you haven't been duped by the investo-tainment hype.

One question that has served me well when I see excessive posturing for a particular stock in the media is: What are other investors thinking about regarding this recent news and how are they going to react to the recent media attention? By thinking socially, I'm in a better position to build my edge and increase the probability of making money from the opportunity.

Improving Your Odds:

In order to become a consistently profitable investor in the stock market, it's important to adhere to a handful of guidelines that increase your chances of success. I keep coming back to this list as a subtle reminder of what I should be doing. And so should you. Here's a half-dozen "golden nuggets" to keep in mind that'll serve you well down the road.

Nugget #1: Always buy the best-of-breed.

Look for businesses that are fundamentally sound. Solid companies offer greater upside potential for you as an investor. Taking the time to check out a handful of potential candidates empowers you by further building your edge in the stock market.

Nugget #2: Try to buy rising stars that are market leaders.

You are in the confidence business. Look for stocks that the big institutional investors have embraced as market leaders. Those stocks with above average trading volume and increasing price appreciation are your natural candidates.

Nugget #3: Become an actively-engaged investor.

By possibly changing your current mindset, so that you go out of your way to seek opportunities will do wonders to your portfolio. This means, disregarding the old buy, hold and forget mentality that is pervasive in today's financial services industry. No park and forget it investing allowed. Be prepared to shift your allocations 6 to 8 times per year as you move from one great opportunity to a better one. Remember, you want to avoid "dead money" investments. Your money has a time value. There is a lost opportunity cost by parking it in a non-performing asset.

Nugget #4: Keep your transaction costs down.

There are many online discount brokers that'll serve your needs well as an active investor. With moving into and out of positions on a regular basis comes the need of having low transaction costs. Keeping more of what you have in your brokerage account is just as important as earning more - they go hand in hand. My advice is to do a comparative analysis of some of the top-rated online discount brokers before moving capital into the markets. Makes a whole lot of sense, right?

Nugget #5: Avoid spontaneous trading & day trading.

You should always have a pre-determined plan of attack for your investment plays. You'll get yourself into more trouble by trying to take advantage of too many opportunities or those spontaneous trades that look very enticing at first glance.

Take the time to do your due diligence by checking out the underlying business and then plan both your entry and exit strategy before diving in. One of the toughest challenges as an investor is resisting the urge to be swept up by the herd mentality that a particular opportunity is a no brainer and that you'll make a lot of money by investing right now. Resist that urge and follow "your" plan.

Nugget #6: Keep an event calendar.

An event calendar helps to remind you of important events and the impact they may have on your investments. What has worked well for me is a daily planner where I can keep track of my trades and highlight specific dates as to when a report may be released. I don't like to spend a lot of time analyzing the data in any one report. I prefer just getting a feel for what the economy may be doing and the direction it may be heading in. As I've mentioned to you in previous chapters, you want a simple investment system that once up and running allows you to make money in the markets with a minimal amount of ongoing monitoring. There should be more to life than the stock market. Does that make sense?

One tool that I have used to keep better track of my investments is **Jeffrey & Yale Hirsch's Stock Trader's Almanac**, which is a yearly strategy calendar with monthly reminders of important dates and events. Their guide has a section at the back for portfolio planning, record keeping and tax preparation. This tool makes it easier to pay attention to cycles and recurring patterns that may have an effect on your buy and sell decisions.

How to Place Your Option Sell Order:

After you have selected the appropriate option strategy that you would like to layer on top of your stock position, you'll need to log into your brokerage account to check out the option premiums available. The list of option strike prices and corresponding premiums is known as the option chain.

Depending on the strategy that you have selected, or will be selecting based on further analysis, you should do an initial calculation of the option return of those 2 or 3 strike prices closest to the current price of the stock. This enables you to have a better perspective of the profitability potential of at least a couple of strike prices.

Look at the current bid price, the lower price, for each option strike price to get a feel for the potential premium you might receive. Ideally, we would like to sell the selected strike price at a price that is between the bid and mid-price for that option. The mid-price is the price half way between the bid and ask prices. Some websites provide this calculation for you or you can simply do the math in your head or "guestimate" the mid price.

Once you have the stock price, the strike prices and the corresponding bid prices, enter this information into an option analysis spreadsheet. A simple spreadsheet can quickly calculate the immediate return that you'll generate from the sale of your option contracts.

The return on your option is calculated by dividing the premium received by the cost basis of your stock. Should you be selling an in-the-money option for some downside protection, the intrinsic value (i.e. protection) is deducted from the option premium before calculating the return. For example, if the stock option is $1 and the stock price is $50, your return on option (ROO) is: $1/($50-$1) = 2.0%.

As previously mentioned the spreadsheet developed by **Owen Sargent** and used extensively by **Alan Ellman** author of **Exit Strategies for Covered Calls** can be downloaded from the Blue Collar Investor website.

It's at this point that you'll need to decide which option strike price that you'll sell. Simply log into your brokerage account and select the specific option that you would like to sell, enter the number of contracts, place a "sell to open" limit order good for the day at a price between the bid and mid prices for the option. Hit the place order button. And check your order status in several minutes.

Once executed (the contracts are sold), record the actual premium that you received in either your trading diary or in a spreadsheet that will track your positions. And should your sell order not be filled as quickly as you would like, go into your brokerage account and "modify" your limit order so that it more closely mirrors the most recent bid price.

Exit Strategies:
To Stop Loss or Not, That is the Question.
I'm often asked if one should use stop loss orders once they purchase their shares of stock in order to protect their downside.

A stop loss order is a limit order that is placed with your online broker to sell a stock when it reaches a particular price, known as the stop price. Once the stock reaches the stop price the order now becomes a market order and will normally be filled at or just below this price.

To determine whether or not you should use this tactic, it would be prudent to assess both the advantages and disadvantages of using a stop loss order. The main advantages to using a stop loss order are that you can:

1. Limit your downside losses to a certain dollar value or percentage of your holding.
2. You have some peace of mind knowing that you can leave your stocks "unattended" for periods of time, for example during an extended vacation, if you are unable to monitor your portfolio.

The major disadvantages are that:

1. You can trigger a sale with a short-term fluctuation in the stock's price by higher than normal buying and selling of the stock. Often the stock price rebounds back up to its previous level within a short period of time. This creates a lost opportunity situation.
2. You can be exposed to losses resulting from a "flash crash", such as the one in May of 2010, where most of the market experienced an intense temporary drop in stock prices. Once again stock prices returned to close to their pre-crash level within a very short period of time. I personally experienced this shocking roller coaster ride with one of my positions. Now I know better after being kicked to the curb. Ouch!
3. You cannot use this tactic if you are trying to stockpile stock as the price goes down. Stockpiling stock is the systematic purchase of blocks of shares over a period of time when there is a pullback in the stock price or a minor correction. This strategy is popular among investors looking to buy their stock at below the fair market value thus creating a margin of safety in the acquisition.
4. You cannot use stop loss orders at the same time as selling your covered calls on stock that you own. Your broker and the types of investment accounts discussed

and used with this guide will not allow you to be in a naked position by selling the underlying security with the calls still being open on the market. There is no longer any collateral (i.e. stock) that covers your call position. This is an extremely risky option position to be in from your broker's perspective, which is why your broker won't go for it.

When deciding whether or not you should use stop loss orders, the real question that you need to ask yourself is: "What is my exit strategy for this particular investment?"

By focusing on the exit strategy first, you're in better control of the possible outcomes. Establishing an exit strategy in advance allows you to use reason not emotions in arriving at your decision.

As an aside, if you're using a growth investment approach or you know in advance that you'll have a short investment period, you may wish to limit your downside losses to 5 to 8%. In which case, a stop loss order may well serve your needs as long as you have not written calls on that particular stock.

I personally do not use stop loss orders, since I try to always layer an option strategy onto my stock positions that I already own.

Now that you have a better perspective of what the pros and cons of stop loss orders can provide, let's examine 10 different times when you could conceivably sell your positions.

Ten Times to Sell Your Stock:
There are many compelling reasons as to why you "could' sell one of your holdings. However, there are few reasons that justify why you really "should" cash out of your position. So, when is an "appropriate" time to sell a stock?

Consider these top 10 reasons why you might close out a position:

Reason #1: Exceptional Stock Growth.
Consider cashing out when your stock has done well and appreciated above your target price, for example having realized a 50% growth in the appreciation of the stock price. It may be appropriate to take some money off of the table and look for the next winning investment.

Reason #2: Poor Business.
If the company fundamentals have changed for the worse and the stock is tanking, you're better off quickly cutting your losses and repositioning your capital. Remember we don't want dead money sitting around. Get out and get into something that has a higher probability of generating better returns.

Reason #3: Poor Performance.
Similar to #2, if you find that the stock is not keeping up with the rest of the market over time and a better opportunity presents itself, jump at it.

Reason #4: Dividend Cuts.
Consider selling any dividend-paying stock if the dividend is cut or eliminated, which may be a red flag that the company will generate less income. Do so only if the general market is not experiencing a major correction.

Reason #5: Can't Sleep.
When you've reached your risk tolerance level and your holding is keeping you up at night, it may be time to liquidate your position and re-evaluate your investment portfolio. I did this with an options play that I was uncomfortable with from the get-go. Despite taking a loss, I was able to sleep better, refocus my energy and find a better opportunity that I was very happy to be in.

Reason #6: Reached Your Goal.

It would be appropriate to move your capital when you've achieved a specific financial goal in the markets and would like to buy a house, fund a college education or build a business.

Reason #7: Opportunity Knocks.

At times, you may need the cash for another investment opportunity such as rental real estate, a systematized business or an angel capital investment. Remember that your focus is on accelerating the velocity of your money from one great opportunity to a better one. Keep an open mind to any and all future possibilities that get you closer to realizing your dreams that much faster.

Reason #8: Retirement.

Should you be in the enviable position to retire, you may wish to shift some of your capital into other assets during retirement or use some of your capital to periodically fund part of your retirement.

Reason #9: Portfolio Out of Whack.

If your stock investment portfolio gets out of balance and you find that you're too heavily weighted in one industry or sector, it may be prudent to sell your position. Reducing your overall portfolio risk should always be in the back of your mind. Preserving your hard-earned capital is paramount.

Reason #10: Unexpected Expense.

As a last resort. you may be faced with an unexpected medical bill or emergency that requires you to liquidate your stock holding. Not an ideal situation to be faced with, but nevertheless an appropriate one should it arise.

There you have it a list of the top 10 times that you may want to consider when selling one of your positions. Your primary objective should be to generate cash flow from better and better investment opportunities. Now that you have an idea as to possible scenarios for selling a particular stock holding, let's take a look at various exit strategies for your covered call positions.

Exit Strategies continued:
Buying to Close a Covered Call Position.

Let's start by taking a look at how you close out an opening position. When you sell a covered call on stock that you own, you enter a "sell to open" transaction on your trading platform.

When you are ready to buy back your position, preferably at a lower price than what you sold the calls for, you enter a "buy to close" order with your online broker. Typically, you will select a limit order that is at the "ask price" or between the ask and the mid-price for that particular option. Recall that the ask price is the higher price between the bid and ask prices posted on the brokerage site. The entire process is the opposite of what you would expect when we sold our options contracts at the lower bid price.

When to Buy-to-Close a Call Position

Here are four guidelines to follow as to when you could place a "buy to close" order:

Guideline #1: Stock is in danger anytime.

Place a "buy to close" order anytime the business shows major weakness in the fundamentals and the stock price could drop dramatically as a result. You want to preserve as much of your hard-earned capital as possible. Therefore, buy back your calls at any price, sell the stock and immediately move the cash into another position that is more deserving from your watch list of potential plays.

Guideline #2: Capture an 80 percent gain within the first couple of weeks.

If the current option premium drops below 20 percent of the initial premium that you received, buy back the contracts. This allows you the opportunity to capture the gains and be in a position to take advantage of another options play opportunity. This opportunity could occur in the same stock as it jumps back in price or it could be with another stock. Remember that the name of the game is cash flow and being able to accelerate your money through the stock market by taking advantage of better and better opportunities.

I like to set a stop loss order for my option contracts at 20% of the initial value that I sold the contracts for. I keep this standing order open until I choose to cancel or modify it. This is the one time that I consistently use stop loss orders - on my option contracts - but not on my stock holdings.

Guideline #3: Capture a 90 percent gain in week 3.

Should the current option premium drop below 10 percent of the original premium paid, close out your position and take your money off of the table. If your contract cycle happens to be 5 weeks long, consider buying back your option position in weeks 3 or 4. With less time left for another option play before contract expiration you should try to capture a little more in profit to compensate for the lack of time remaining. A reasonable level is to increase your expectation from 80 to 90 percent.

At the beginning of week 3, I like to reset (modify) my option stop-loss orders to reflect the new 10 percent limit. I usually keep the stop loss order "good until the close" GTC on expiration Friday.

Guideline #4: Change in stock or market tone in week 4.
There may be times when circumstances dictate that the prudent course of action is to close out your option position during the last week of the option cycle rather than do nothing and wait. You may feel that it's necessary to close out your position if the market tone changes quickly.

Should the stock show signs of weakness in its fundamentals and technicals, you might be better off exiting your position right away rather than waiting until expiration Friday. You'll want to try and convert potentially dead money into cash as soon as possible.

On the flip side, the stock may have appreciated in price above your previously sold strike price and you would like to hang onto it rather than have it called away by expiration Friday. By closing your position and simultaneously selling the next month's strike generally at or above the current stock price you can maintain control over your position.

This is the subject of the next section. Now that we have an idea as to how to close out your option positions, let's take a look at the concept of "rolling" your contracts.

Rolling Positions from One Month to the Next.
Rolling is a common option exit strategy whereby you close out your current position and immediately sell another position. This is typically done part way through the current month's option contract with the sale of option contracts set up for the next month.

There are three different rolling strategies, namely:
1. Rolling down.
2. Rolling out (also known as rolling forward).
3. Rolling out and up.

Let's walk through a case study for each strategy to give you an idea as to how you can use them as part of your arsenal of timing strategies available.

Strategy #1: Rolling down case study.
This particular strategy is used when the price of your stock has dropped. The signals triggering this move might be an overall market tone that is mixed to negative with the stock's technicals indicating a downward trend in price movement.

Rolling down allows you to close out your current position taking a profit on the sale of your current month's option contracts. You then sell the next month's strike price that is lower than your current month's strike; hence, the term rolling down. The upside is that you benefit from both option sales.

Of course, the downside is that your stock has dropped in price and you now have a potential loss to deal with. However, the options premiums received offset some, if not all, of the decline in the stock price. Your option premiums received have reduced your cost basis in your stock providing you with some downside protection. This strategy is a far better alternative than waiting for a rebound in the stock price had you not used an option strategy.

It's mid-2018 as I write this book and the markets have had a couple of wild swings. I'm subtly reminded once again as to the wealth building power of option selling. Despite a couple of my equity holdings losing "paper value", I'm still capable of generating monthly income. As long as I control blocks of 100 shares, I can write covered calls and make money even if the stocks have lost value on paper. Now that's powerful, wouldn't you concur?

Eventually, stock prices will trend back up to their former level. What's reassuring is the ability to still generate income even with a holding that has supposedly "lost" value. If I were a typical buy and hold investor, my stress level would be through the roof since I would have to wait until my holdings had climbed back up to get me back to even.

Let's take a quick look at a specific example of how the rolling down strategy might play out in the real world.

Let's say you pick up shares of O'Reilly Automotive that you bought in early June for $98. At the time of the purchase ORLY checked out in the fundamental and technical departments as being a potential investment play. You also have noted that the company has scheduled to release its quarterly earnings report on July 25 five days after expiration Friday for the July option cycle.

Logging into your brokerage account, you decide to select a slightly in-the-money (ITM) July (95) strike price. You enter a limit order between the bid and mid-price for the option and manage to sell the call for $5.75 giving you an immediate profit from the cash flow of almost 6 percent and roughly 3 percent should the stock get called away. Not a bad start to the month.

Unfortunately, about 2 weeks later, O'Reilly issues a warning about an earnings shortfall. This news hammers the stock dropping 18 percent to $79.16. Your immediate reaction might be to panic. However, unlike a buy and hold investor, you have some powerful weapons in your arsenal. Your objective now is damage control and mitigating your losses.

A little over a week later in early July, you decide to use an option strategy to decrease your unfortunate "potential" loss in the stock. Let's assume that the stock had rebounded from its initial bottom of $79.16 to $86.74. You notice that you could "buy to close" the

July (95) call for $0.15 at the ask price. You do so which generates a "realized" option return of $5.60 per contract.

You can now take a look at Augusts' (the next month's) option chain to see if you can reduce your losses. In looking at Augusts' option chain, you decide to roll down to a lower strike and "sell to open" the August (90) call for $2.05. You do so by placing a sell order between the bid and mid prices for the option.

First off, you'll notice that the current stock price of $86.74 is below the August (90) strike price and therefore won't get called away as of the current date.

The total premium received for this month is made up of the sale of the July (95) call plus the August (90) call less the cost of closing the July (95) call. This amounts to $7.65 per share or $765 per contract written (i.e. $575 + $205 - $15).

Your "potential" stock price loss should you not use an option strategy is equal to your initial purchase price of $98.00 less the current stock price of $86.74 leaving you with a loss of $11.26 per share or $1126 per 100 shares. This represents a potential loss of 11.5 percent.

Using your option strategy, the new cost basis in the stock drops by $765 (total premiums) from $9800 (initial stock price) to $9035 or $90.35 per share. Your potential loss in the stock, which is the difference between the new cost basis of $90.35 and the current stock price of $86.74, is $3.61 per share or $361 for each option contract. This represents only a 3.6 percent drop versus almost 12 percent had you not used any options strategies.

One downside that I should point out in using this particular strategy is that you do not know how the market will react to the actual earnings report announcement scheduled just after expiration Friday in July.

On the upside, you still have some time to determine which exit strategy to employ prior to expiration Friday in August. At least in the interim you've reduced the serious effects of a hefty stock price drop.

Note that should your stock close out the month just above your August (90) strike, your loss when the stock is called away (sold), has been reduced to $35 which is less than 1 percent. This was calculated by comparing the 90 strike to the new cost basis in the stock which you reduced to $90.35 from your options plays. At the end of the day on expiration Friday your broker would deposit $9000 into your brokerage account from the sale of your stock. The difference of 35 cents or $35 for each contract represents your actual loss for the period.

This example illustrates that not all options plays will be financially rewarding. The stark reality about investing is that unforeseen circumstances can factor into your ability to come out on top with each and every investment opportunity. The good news is that you have a handful of effective strategies to fall back on that'll minimize the impact of such unanticipated situations. You now can quickly get back to even despite a major hit to the stock. That is the important lesson to take away from this particular case study. Options can reduce your potential losses and get you back to even faster.

Another strategy to consider, should the stock recover from the initial shock and begin to rise up to your 90 strike, is that of rolling out or forward to the next month, which is the topic of discussion that follows.

Strategy #2: Rolling out (forward) case study.

This strategy is often used when the stock price has appreciated in value up to the previously sold strike price or may even be slightly higher than the strike price. The signals triggering this move might be an overall market tone that is mixed to positive and the stock's technicals may be showing the same signs.

If we deem that this is a stock that we would like to hang onto into the future because of either the dividends it generates or the stock's price appreciation potential, then rolling out makes sense.

To roll out, you would close your current position by buying back the contracts and then simultaneously, sell the next month's contracts with the same strike price. This is usually either an in-the-money (ITM) or an at-the-money (ATM) call.

In all likelihood, the current price of the stock will be slightly above your next month's strike. In other words, you will be selling an in-the-money (ITM) call giving you both a good premium and some downside protection. The downside protection is created as a result of the difference between the stock's current price being slightly higher than the ITM strike price being sold.

Let's assume that you bought 400 shares of Eli Lilly symbol LLY for $41.99 in early June. Eli Lilly is a well-established manufacturer of drugs with global exposure. It has rewarded its shareholders with generous dividends, with projected annual yields of around 4 percent. At the time of the purchase, the stock had an earnings report due 4 days after expiration Friday on July 25.

The initial strategy selected for this stock was to capture primarily the price appreciation occurring in the market by selling an out-of-the-money July call. Four July (44) contracts were sold in anticipation that the stock will continue its upward climb on good earnings from the last quarter. The contracts were sold at a little better than the bid price for $0.23 per share.

This generates an immediate cash flow of $92 into your brokerage account, which represents an immediate return of about 1 percent. Not much in terms of an immediate return. However, should the stock get called away at the July (44) strike, this would generate a return of 5.4 percent for the roughly 7-week time period (since we bought the shares and sold the contracts in mid-June).

About one month later in mid- July, Eli Lilly had appreciated up to the July (44) strike. The current stock price 3 days prior to expiration Friday is $43.96 with a very good chance of it being called away. It's time to re-think your exit strategy should you still want to hang onto the stock for its rich dividend.

Were you to simply wait for the stock to be called away, you would benefit from a 5.4 percent return. However, if you felt that the stock still had some upside potential and you wanted to capture the September dividend payment, then rolling forward to the next month makes sense.

Let's assume that the ex-date for receiving the dividend is August 13th, with the record date being August 15th. Recall that your "must own" date is 3 days prior to the record date which is the 12th. Holding onto the stock past the middle of August allows you to receive some additional cash flowing into your brokerage account mid-September when the dividend is actually issued.

Knowing that earnings will be announced on July 25th just after Julys' expiration Friday date poses a challenge. Do we take the prudent course of action and let the stock be called away should it rise above the 44 strike, or are we confident in our analysis that the company is still a positive grower?

If you like what you see in the long-term potential of the business and the current fundamentals support that position, then rolling forward is a viable option. The one caveat is that you must accept the responsibility of closely monitoring your position around the earnings announcement.

Let's see how rolling forward could play out for the month of August. The first order of business is to close out your previous calls by buying back the options at or near the ask price. For this case study let's say that you have to pay $0.48 per share or $192 (for 4 contracts). You've now bought up the value in the stock from your initial price of $41.99 to the current price of $43.96.

The next step is to immediately sell next month's same strike, thereby rolling forward your position. Selling at or near the bid would bring in $1.32 in immediate cash.

First off, you'll notice that the current stock price of $43.96 is below the August (44) strike price and therefore won't get called away as of the current date.

The total premium received for this month is made up of the sale of the July (44) call plus the August (44) call less the cost of closing the July (44) call (i.e. $0.23 + $1.32 - $0.48). This amounts to $1.07 per share or $428 (i.e. $1.07 x 400 shares), which provides a total return including the price appreciation of the stock for the roughly 2-month period of 7.4 percent.

Given that you're eligible to capture the next dividend of say $0.49 or $196 this increases your total potential return to 8.7 percent and all within a 2-month window.

Recall that your initial goal was to capture the upside growth in the price appreciation of the stock. As the month played out you were able to see that the company did in fact reach your target expectation. The choice that you'll often be faced with is do I take money off the table right away or let it ride a little longer for another month.

If you did nothing in July and the stock closes above the July (44) strike it will be called away (i.e. sold) and you'll have cash in your account ready for the next opportunity. The actual total return for the 6-week period would be 5.7 percent. Not a bad return, wouldn't you agree?

If you did nothing in July and the stock closes below the July (44) strike, you're free to wait until after the July 25th earnings report and then pop into the market with an appropriate call strategy or sell the stock and move into a better opportunity altogether.

A downside of using this "wait and see" approach is that your call option growth strategy generates a minimal amount of cash flowing immediately into your account. Therefore, you must be willing to accept the risk of generating a lower return on your investment capital when you initially sell your calls, which occurred in mid-June. By using a growth strategy you're hoping that you'll make the majority of your money when the stock price appreciates up to or past the strike.

On the flip side, if you're confident in your analysis of the stock and the market and you would prefer holding onto the stock as a future cash cow, then using the rolling out strategy is one viable option. Rolling out generates more upfront cash into your brokerage account as opposed to waiting and hoping.

My intent with this case study was to share with you some ways of moving into and out of the stock market depending on your specific objectives at the time. By analyzing the cash production potential of various scenarios, you'll be more effective in generating a consistent stream of cash flowing into your brokerage account.

Should the stock continue to rise up past your 44 strike, then you can always use the next strategy being discussed that of rolling out and up for the next month. Let's now take a look at our final exit strategy that of rolling out and up.

Strategy #3: Rolling out and up case study.

This strategy is used when the stock price has appreciated beyond your previously sold strike price and you would like to hang onto the stock anticipating further price appreciation. The signals triggering this move might be a stock and a market tone that are positive both in terms of the stock's fundamentals and the technicals for the market and the stock.

To roll out and up you would close out your current position by buying back the option contracts. Then you would sell the next month's higher strike contracts. This could conceivably be an at-the-money (ATM) strike or an out-of-the-money (OTM) strike depending on how much the stock price has risen.

You buy back the value of your stock by first closing the previous position and then selling the next month's higher strike. The resulting transaction is that your net result of buying and selling option contracts plus the increased equity value that you bought up results in an overall return that is higher. Had you done nothing you would have probably been exercised on expiration Friday and received just the option premium for your efforts had the strike been at-the-money.

Let's assume that you purchased Oracle shares in late June at $28.05 per share with a total of 400 shares being purchased. On the same day, you sold 4 at-the-money ATM covered call option contracts with a July (28) strike for $1.00 each giving you an immediate cash deposit of $400. Let's also assume that your initial strategy was to use a pure income play and that you expected the stock to be called away at the end of July should it stay above the 28 strike.

This income strategy represents an immediate return of 3.6 percent, which falls into our monthly sweet spot zone of 2 to 4 percent. July happens to be a 5-week option cycle month, so we would expect to lean towards an option return that is closer to 4 percent rather than 2 percent given that the extra week that can work against us as sellers of options.

You'll also notice that 400 shares were bought allowing you to write 4 option contracts thereby reducing your overall transaction fees per contract sold. Recall that whenever possible you always try to purchase a 400 or 500 block of shares to help reduce your call option transaction fees.

Let's say that Oracle has been trading in a price range between 25 and 34 for the past year. The company also had a favorable quarterly earnings report announcement in late June, the day before the shares were purchased.

Let's assume that by mid-July, Oracle has appreciated 5.5 percent in price from $28.05 to $29.58. In all likelihood, the stock will be called away come expiration Friday in one week's time. If you now decide to modify your exit strategy and hold onto the stock capturing some of this price appreciation, you would use a roll out and up strategy. As well, with a dividend-paying stock like Oracle it may be of benefit to try and capture any upcoming dividend payments in addition to the covered call premiums.

The first order of business is to close out your initial July (28) strike by buying back the contracts. In this case they were bought back for $1.64, which was the current asking price for the contracts. Buying back the July (28) contracts, in effect buys back the equity in the stock. Once again you would do this by logging into your brokerage account and placing a limit order close to the ask price for the option. If your limit price has not been exercised within a short period of time, go back and modify your order.

Of course, you can always place a market order to close out your position faster, as opposed to a limit order. This decision should be based on how much time you want to devote to closing and opening your contracts and your comfort level with moving into and out of positions. Sometimes, placing a market order ensures that you move into and out of positions with fewer hassles and greater peace of mind. Choose the approach that you're most comfortable with at the time of the transaction.

You would then select a higher strike price for the next month's option contract, preferably just above the current price of the stock. In this case study an August (31) call, which is out-of-the money would be selected since the stock is currently trading at $29.58.

To summarize, you're using the combination of buying and selling the option contracts to capture the price appreciation in the stock price and set yourself up for some additional upside potential.

First off, you'll notice that the current stock price of $29.58 is below the August (31) strike price and therefore won't get called away as of the current date.

The total premium received for this month is made up of the sale of the July (28) call plus the August (31) call less the cost of closing the July (28) call. Your total premium generated for July is going to be a slight loss (i.e. $1.00 + $0.21 - $1.64 = -$0.43). This amounts to a loss of $0.43 per share or $172.

This amount is what you would have paid out of your brokerage account to buy back the value in the stock. We have now benefited from the stock price appreciation which has gone from $28.05 to $29.58. This represents a 3.9 percent net increase after factoring in the cost of buying back the equity. The maximum upside potential for this combination of strategies should the stock close above the August (31) strike is 9.0 percent over roughly a nine-week period of time.

By using the rolling out and up strategy you can position yourself to take advantage of the price appreciation potential of the stock. This strategy is an important one to employ when you would like to hang onto the stock for either the dividends it is paying out or the potential upside appreciation in the stock price.

In our example, Oracle will pay a quarterly dividend of $0.06 in early August, which is between our two option contract monthly cycles. This amounts to an additional $24 being deposited into your brokerage account, giving you a potential maximum return of 9.2 percent over that 2-month period of time. Now that's better than a poke in the eye with a sharp stick.

Recall that your initial intent was to capture the 3.6 percent call premium up front and be willing to let the stock be called away since you were using a pure income generation play. However, sometimes by rolling up and out you can hang onto those dividend-paying stocks that are also trending upwards.

This case study illustrates the point that by taking an active role in your investing you're able to take better advantage of opportunities as they unfold. You may enter the market using one cash generation strategy only to find out after the fact that a more lucrative position can be created.

As a smart investor take some time to analyze if a potentially better opportunity could be unfolding with your positions, then make the judgment call as to whether it is more advantageous to switch to a different exit strategy or stay the course with your initial decision. Having an arsenal of different exit strategies to choose from empowers you to be a better cash flow generation machine in the stock market, wouldn't you agree?

In the above case study, should the stock and the market as a whole show technical signs of leveling out then switching from your growth strategy to a pure income play for the following month of September may be the way to go. Should the stock begin to trade sideways selling ATM calls for the immediate income optimizes the cash flowing into your account.

And should the stock and the market as a whole continue their upward climb using a growth strategy is a good option. No pun intended. You not only capture the immediate premium but you also have some stock price appreciation potential built in.

In general, my personal preference is to optimize my immediate cash flow into my brokerage account which can then be allocated when I see investment opportunities unfolding. So, I have a tendency to write more ATM calls than OTM calls.

The following action steps summarize when you could conceivably employ the various exit strategies discussed.

Action Step #1: Take no action.

If no advantage may be gained and there have been no changes in the fundamentals or technicals.

Action Step #2: Close your option position.

Lock in your profits and wait for another option play on the same stock. Buy back your contracts in the first 2 weeks when you have a gain of 80%. Buy back your contracts during the 3rd week if you see a 90% gain.

Action Step $3: Close your option position and sell your stock.

Do so if the stock is no longer fundamentally sound or the stock market is in danger.

Action Step #4: Roll down your position.

If your stock declines in price and you still want to keep it (possibly for a dividend payout).

Action Step #5: Roll out your position.

If your stock price is now greater than your initial purchase price as you approach expiration Friday and you would like to keep the holding. Do so if you have a neutral outlook for the market.

Action Step #6: Roll out and up.

If your stock price is now greater than your initial purchase price as you approach expiration Friday and you would like to keep the holding. Do so if you have a bullish outlook for the market.

Your overall objective is to use exit strategies to make money and to minimize potential losses.

Having walked through several examples of various timing strategies that you can employ, you may have noticed that there are preferential conditions where certain strategies work better than others. As an actively-engaged investor you can take advantage of those conditions and increase your probability of generating superior returns in the stock market.

Basic Timing Guideline:

The following is a simple guideline that I use for my investment decisions that may prove useful to you. These numbers are not carved in stone; however, they do provide you with a starting point from which to base your decisions as to which strategy may be the most appropriate. Play with the numbers as you see fit depending on your comfort level for risk, your current skill set and the time that you realistically have available for your investing.

My simple approach looks at what the monthly appreciation is for the S&P 500. I like to use the SPY ETF for my analysis, as follows:

1. If >3% = Hold onto your stock and rub your hands together like a giddy child.
2. 1% to 3% = Sell OTM calls - focus on growth.
3. Flat ± 1% = Sell ATM calls or ITM calls - focus on income.
4. -1% to -3% = Sell ITM calls - focus on protection.
5. < -3% = Move to cash &/or Buy a dividend stock.

You've now been empowered to become a better investor. This chapter should provide you with a boost of additional confidence that'll help you achieve your financial dreams that much faster. Wouldn't that be awesome?

Chapter 9 - Structuring Your Stock Investment Portfolio

Focus Questions:
1. What should I be doing on a daily basis to keep tabs on my stock holdings?
2. How should I go about monitoring my portfolio's performance?
3. What should I invest in when first starting out?
4. How should I structure my stock investment portfolio?
5. Where should I focus my attention over the next couple of years?

Your last chapter focuses on how you can tie all of the concepts that we've discussed thus far into a systematic investment process. You'll be able to follow this process over the next couple of years as you evolve as an investor in being the best that you can become.

Your Daily Routine:
Before we explore how you can structure your stock investment portfolio and where you should focus your attention over the next couple of years, let's look at a simple daily routine for monitoring your positions.

Ideally, you'll want to check on your positions twice a day. Taking 10 - 15 minutes in the morning and at the end of the day should keep you abreast of what is happening in the market and hopefully keep you out of any serious trouble.

First things first. After you've had your green drink smoothie, tall glass of water or cup of java in the morning, log into your online broker account. Ah coffee! The sweet balm by which many of us accomplish tasks. Sorry, I digress. You could also check out how the overall markets are doing at websites such as FinViz or Yahoo Finance.

Step #1: Review the overall market sentiment and any global news that may affect your current holdings.
Step #2: Review the news for each stock that you're holding. If the news is positive, think about how you could capture any gains. And if the news is negative, consider an appropriate exit strategy. Also check each stock's technical chart to verify if there were any gaps overnight that could affect your current strategy.
Step #3: Take any appropriate action if need be.
Step #4: Towards the end of the trading day around 3:30 PM EST, review the news to see if there is anything negative that might affect your positions. If you're unable to do so right before the markets close, at least verify how your holdings are doing later that evening.
Step #5: Take a quick look at a technical chart for each stock to make sure that they're behaving according to your trading plan.
Step #6: Take any appropriate action if need be. Depending on what the situation is, you may wish to wait a day or so to see if it resolves itself.

Your Quarterly Review:
Ever stop to think and forget to start again? You may be wondering about how you should go about monitoring your progress in your stock portfolios. Your online discount broker may be posting the daily change in your portfolio like mine does.

For the most part, I ignore this data. I'm not too concerned about knowing the day-to-day changes that occur. What I'm more interested in is the monthly flow of cash that occurs. And since this flow moves like an ocean wave, I look at my quarterly progress.

There are two metrics I'm most interested in. The first is how much cash I've been able to generate during the quarter from my options plays. In other words, what is the return on my options (ROO). Not only do I like to know if my portfolio is generating a decent return of hopefully 2 - 3%, I'm also interested in the dollar value that's associated with this return.

The second metric that I like to track is the income generated from my dividend stocks for that quarter. And the third piece of helpful information is the overall value of my portfolio. Has it appreciated in value over the quarter or lost some ground?

Keep in mind that the stock market moves up and down over the course of a week or month not unlike an ocean wave. This is why checking your portfolio performance on a quarterly basis makes more sense than a daily or weekly assessment.

Recall that when you control a number of options contracts, you can still generate a positive flow of cash into your brokerage account despite having a portfolio of stocks that have lost some "book" value. It's not until you sell those shares that you actually realize a loss.

This notion is encouraging because it illustrates that you can make money in the stock market despite the market going through a short correction period. A case in point is one of my own portfolios that lost book value in early 2018, yet I was able to continue having a positive cash flow with my options contracts. Wouldn't you feel more confident if this scenario played out for your portfolio?

Now, let's explore how you could structure your overall portfolios and where to focus your attention over the next couple of years in setting up your cash flow machine. Ready to get started?

Phase One: Building Your Core Positions.
Objectives:
Your primary objective in phase one is to build a core position of 6 holdings that are diversified across a minimum of 5 industries. You may even want to consider adding a broad-based index fund like the S&P 500 (SPY) that'll allow you to write covered calls as part of the mix. As you're building your core positions strive to become comfortable using the various cash flow strategies through both paper-trading and with money on the line.

Process:
Your first task is to find and assess 10 to 20 potential watch list candidates across various sectors. For you "keeners" try to create a watch list of 30 to 40 possible candidates. What I've found is that the more research I do up front while my enthusiasm is still high, the longer the pay-off down the road. By creating a broad watch list, you open up that many more doors. If you have the time and the conviction go for it.

You have a number of approaches that I have presented for finding and assessing potential candidates. I prefer using the screening tools offered by some of the expert authors on their websites to generate a potential list. This has saved me some time when I got started in the game.

I then verify the key growth rates by visiting any of the free financial websites that report on individual stocks. I like to plug in the 7, 5, 3 and one year values for return on invested capital, earnings per share, sales, book value per share, and cash flow into my spreadsheet to give me a quick snapshot of how the business is growing.

Having read this book up to this point, you now have a solid foundation of the key concepts to consider when looking for great stocks. Whether or not you use all of them or just a handful in your selection process is a personal choice. What's important is that you're aware of those factors that have a significant impact on a business's ability to become a market leader and best of breed in its class.

After you have a list of fundamentally sound businesses to work with the next step is to select your specific holdings.

To build your core positions start by buying one growth dividend-paying stock. Then buy one market leader that you can sell covered calls on. Rinse and repeat this process for a total of 3 times giving you 6 holdings. If possible, try to identify dividend-paying stocks that have different quarterly payment dates so that you can create a more consistent annual cash flow from your initial three core holdings.

As you invest your capital, keep in mind what sectors are currently in favor and have a tailwind pushing stock prices higher. Avoid bucking the trend and investing in sectors that are not trending higher. This can be easily done by checking out a 3 to 6-month technical chart of each of the eleven sector SPDRs.

The objective is to accelerate your cash flow, not to sit, wait and pray for a particular stock to begin trending higher sometime in the future. Remember dead money does you no good as an actively-engaged investor. I'm always amazed at how many great investment opportunities are just waiting for the retail investor to ride up to higher levels if you look for them.

Core Position Building Benefits:
The top four benefits of setting up your initial portfolio are:

1. The three dividend-paying stocks provide a monthly dividend cash flow to be used or re-invested as opportunities present themselves.
2. The three covered call positions provide monthly premiums.
3. You're mitigating your risk by diversifying across a minimum of 5 sectors.
4. You've just created a manageable cash flow portfolio.

Time frame:
You should be able to build your portfolio of core positions with a conservative allocation of your capital over 2 years. Given that each holding could represent a minimum cash outlay of $2000 to $4000 you would probably want to budget for $20,000 to $40,000 for your core positions. This is a do-able objective for most over a 2-year time frame.

For the investor with an "aggressive" allocation of capital, consider a time-frame of 6 to 12 months for the initial allocation of your capital.

Frequently Asked Questions:
Here are five most frequently asked questions novice investors ask when they are beginning to build their core positions:
Question #1: What is the minimum I should invest in order to build an initial position?
Try to invest the minimum amount of capital so that the brokerage fees represent less than 1% of your capital outlay. For example, if you are paying $10 in online brokerage transaction fees for a small stock purchase, try to invest at least $1000. When you're starting out, fees can eat away at your potential returns. If at all possible, try to pick up round lots of 100 shares of stock so that you can write covered calls on all of the stock being held at some

point in the future. This exposes 100 percent of your shares to each opportunity thereby optimizing your potential returns.

Question #2: Which sector should I invest in first?
Start by looking for a dividend-paying company that is in the consumer staples sector. Many of these mature businesses tend to be steady consistent growers over time. Another consideration is to select an exchange traded fund (ETF) that allows you to write covered calls.

Question #3: What should my first stock pick for covered calls be?
Find a business you're already familiar with and that you would enjoy learning a little more about from a business perspective. Remember it is much easier for you to do your homework on a business that you would enjoy exploring than a business you know absolutely nothing about.

Question #4: Into which industries or sectors should I first diversify?
Consider having holdings in the following industries to start:
- Consumer staples.
- Energy.
- Financials.
- Precious metals (if not holding bullion).
- Health Care or Consumer Discretionary.

Question #5: I'm not sure about how to use the various strategies presented. What do you recommend?
Start paper trading right away. Paper trading is exactly the same as the real McCoy except that no money is actually invested. You keep track of your transactions on paper or by using an electronic spreadsheet. Several online brokers also offer paper-trading platforms or practice accounts that allow you to hone your skills

before investing a penny. This is a great way to get into trading options and learning how to use the various strategies discussed in this guide.

Phase Two: Diversifying Across Cash Flow Strategies.
Objectives:
During phase two you're looking at consistent ways to increase your monthly cash flow by using the various cash flow strategies presented. As well, you'll want to expand the total number of holdings at any one time from 6 to 10 thereby increasing your diversification and opportunities.

During any one month, you may see the following cash flow scenarios develop:
- 1 or 2 dividend payments being made to your account.
- 1 or 2 covered call positions on those dividend stocks paying a monthly premium.
- 5 or 6 other covered call positions paying premiums.

Process:
As you become more comfortable with the various call option strategies, you'll begin to shift your portfolio emphasis to using call options while maintaining a core position of dividend-paying stocks. One possible shift to consider is moving from growth to income dividend-paying stocks.

Cash Flow Strategy Diversification Benefits:
The top three strategy diversification benefits are:
1. You become adept at making money with a variety of cash flow strategies not just one. This flexibility improves your odds of coming out on top of a winning trade. You're now focusing on accelerating your cash flow.
2. By diversifying across a minimum of 5 industries and 3 or 4 cash flow strategies you not only minimize various types of

risk associated with investing, but you're also better poised to take advantage of opportunities as they present themselves.

3. And last, but not least, you'll build your skill set to be able to consistently make money in various market conditions whether the market is trending higher or not.

Time frame:

Phase two can be realistically be achieved by the "mere mortal" in 6 to 12 months. On the other hand, for those "keeners" out there, a 3 to 6-month time period is do-able.

Frequently Asked Questions:

Here are the answers to four frequently asked questions about using the cash flow strategies:

Question #1: Which covered call strategy should I use first?
The most popular covered call strategy is selling out-of-the money (OTM) calls. This strategy as you recall focuses more on stock price appreciation and growth of the underlying security as opposed to income generation with an at-the-money (ATM) call.

Being the most popular does not necessarily mean that this is where you should focus your efforts. Rather, look at what the market and the stock in particular are telling you and then pick an appropriate strategy. You may find that a pure income generation approach may be best suited for optimizing your cash flow.

Question #2: How much cash should I have on the sidelines?
Opportunities present themselves at a moment's notice. It's always a good idea to have cash available on the sidelines to take advantage of these time-sensitive opportunities. Consider setting aside at least enough money to cover the cost of purchasing 100 shares of stock down the road. You should also have cash on hand in your brokerage account in order to effectuate some of the

exit strategies presented, so that you can optimize your overall returns. I usually allocate a minimum of 5% for potential exit strategies. You may wish to do the same.

Question #3: Why go from growth to income producing dividends?

As you become a better cash flow investor, you may discover that you can accelerate your cash flow potential by using income-producing strategies as opposed to growth strategies with dividend-paying stocks. This transition may occur when you find that your monthly covered call strategies produce more consistent and profitable results. With time, you'll discover how to best time moving into and out of positions in order to optimize your profits.

Question #4: How much time do I realistically need to manage my portfolio?

Once you have spent some initial time developing a watch list of great stocks, the weekly maintenance on your investments should decrease. A portfolio of 10 holdings should require no more than a few hours during the week and on the weekend assuming that you're comfortable moving into and out of brokerage accounts and informational websites in order to do your "weekly" homework.

Whether you're spending 5 hours per week or 15 is not the critical question to ask. The most important question to ask when you're assessing how you spend your time pursuing one activity over another is: Is what I am doing, bringing me closer to realizing my dreams, or not?

We all have choices to make with how we spend our time. Choose to allocate enough time to create the wealth that you would like through your investments.

Phase Three: Playing to Your Strengths.
Objectives:

At some point in time you'll want to move towards systematizing your investment plays so that you spend less time making more money. This can be accomplished through the use of better investment platforms or investment services that streamline the information flow so that you can make faster decisions and easily track your performance. Your ultimate goal with your investing should be to create a time-rich lifestyle in which you're able to pursue your dream lifestyle on your terms.

Process:

In order to play to your strengths, you'll need to re-balance your portfolio holdings to take advantage of your skill set and proven track record. This will require that you engage in a personal assessment of your investing prowess. Start by doing a self-evaluation of those investment strategies that have been the easiest for you to employ weighed against the cash flow potential being generated. Consider how effective you use your time in producing your desired level of cash flow.

Another task that you'll want to undertake is to explore what other experts have to offer in the way of products or services that'll drastically reduce the amount of time completing any of the FAST steps. The FAST steps are those specific tasks that find and assess potential businesses, implement investment strategies or optimize the timing of your entry and exit into the market.

Playing to Your Strengths Benefits:

The top two benefits of playing to your specific strengths as an investor are:
1. Psychologically, you become a more confident investor and trader. As your confidence grows, you increase the consistency of producing winning trades.

2. You reduce your overall portfolio risk by focusing on what works best for you as an investor. Remember, it's your financial intelligence that determines if you're exposing yourself to increased risk or not. As your investment knowledge and skill set grows over time, your ability to generate double-digit returns while mitigating various types of risk also grows as well.

Time frame:
A reasonable time frame for the mere mortal to aspire to for this phase of your portfolio structuring is 6 to 12 months and for you "keeners" 3 to 6 months.

Frequently Asked Questions:
The last four frequently asked questions for tapping into your strengths as an investor are:
Question #1: Is it okay to just sell covered calls?
The short answer: yes. The bottom line is that you may find that as an investor you're more adept at producing the cash flow that you require from just writing covered calls. If you're playing to your strengths then this would be the logical course of action.

The whole purpose of this book is to present you with some of the best time-tested cash flow strategies used today that you can have fun playing with and then select those strategies that resonate with you the most. How much better would that be?

Question #2: Whose stock investing tools/ services can I trust?
When I look for third-party products or services in the stock investing world, I always come back to one key question: Does the provider add value to investors as a whole by providing free educational material or does the provider just have a marketing platform for their product or service? My word of advice is to spend a little time exploring the provider's website to see if what

they're offering makes sense to you as a tool or service. Is it going to save you time and eventually make you more money? Ultimately, you want to be able to spend less time dealing with your investments and more time pursuing your dream lifestyle. Does that make sense?

Question #3: What is a realistic portfolio return objective?
My advice is to work over the next 1 to 2 years at becoming a confident cash flow investor capable of consistently doubling your investment capital every 3 to 4 years. This means that you should strive to not only beat the market averages but to also position yourself for consistent double-digit growth for many years to come.

Question #4: How do I grow beyond what this book has to offer?
My simple advice is to always remain a consummate learner, seeking answers to your most pressing questions. Continue to search for those answers on free internet sites.

Failing that - look for programs or services that are going to challenge your overall growth as an investor. Skill development will only take you so far. Also consider having a coach or mentor in your corner who'll move you to your next level faster.

I'm often reminded of this inspirational quote: Life is like a roll of toilet paper. The closer it gets to the end, the faster it goes.

The choice is yours right now. You can let life happen to you. Or you can embrace the wealth of insights, advice and strategies in this book and begin building life on your terms. I hope that you choose to take action today and begin increasing the velocity of your money in the stock market. If you mastered some of these skills, where would you be 5 years from now. Ready to get started?

Review Request:

Before you go, I'd like to thank you for investing in my guide. I know that you could have picked from dozens of books on covered call writing and stock investing, but you took a chance with my system. So, a big thank you for purchasing this book and reading all the way to the end.

If you enjoyed this book or if you found that you have gained greater insights into how you could conceivably build a better lifestyle, then I'd be very grateful if you'd post a positive review.

Your support really does matter and it really does make a difference. The feedback and encouragement will help me continue to write the kind of books that help you get results.

If you'd like to leave a review then all you need to do is go to the customer review section on the book's Amazon page. You'll then see a big button that says: "Write a customer review" - click that and you're good to go.

Thanks again for your support. To your ongoing success as a cash flow investor.

Randall

30 Resources to Explore:

Here is a list of the majority of the resources that I've used over the years to help me become a better investor. Some of these are classic guides that have stood the test of time. Should something tickle your fancy, check out those topics that may be of interest.

The DNA of Success by Jack Zufelt
Publisher: Z Publishing (2003)
Paperback: 208 pages

Succeed: How We Can Reach Our Goals by Dr. Heidi Grant Halverson
Publisher: Hudson Street Press (2010)
Hardcover: 288 pages

Secrets of the Millionaire Mind by T. Harv Eker
Publisher: Harper Business (2005)
Hardcover: 224 pages

Power of Focus by Jack Canfield, Mark Victor Hansen and Les Hewitt
Publisher: HCI (2000)
Paperback: 310 pages

The Power Curve by Scott Kyle
Publisher: Nautilus Press (2009)
Hardcover: 256 pages

Trading in the Zone by Mark Douglas
Publisher: Prentice Hall Press (January 1, 2001)
Hardcover: 240 pages

Market Mind Games by Denise Shull
Publisher: McGraw-Hill (2011)
Hardcover: 288 pages

Rich Dad's Guide to Investing by Robert Kiyosaki
Publisher: Time Warner Books (2000)
Paperback: 403 pages

The Millionaire Next Door: The Surprising Secrets of America's Wealthy by Thomas Stanley & William Danko
Publisher: Taylor Trade Publishing (2010)
Paperback: 272 pages

The Millionaire Maker: Act, Think, and Make Money the Way the Wealthy Do by Loral Langemeier
Publisher: McGraw-Hill (2005)
Hardcover: 240 pages

Rich Dad's Advisors: Guide to Investing In Gold and Silver: Protect Your Financial Future by Michael Maloney
Publisher: Business Plus (2008)
Paperback: 240 pages

Getting Back to Even: Your Personal Economic Recovery Plan by James J. Cramer
Publisher: Simon & Schuster (2009)
Hardcover: 352 pages

The Little Book of Big Dividends: A Safe Formula for Guaranteed Returns by Charles B. Carlson
Publisher: John Wiley & Sons (2010)
Hardcover: 174 pages

Options Trading for the Conservative Investor: Increasing Profits without Increasing Risk by Michael C. Thomsett
Publisher: Prentice Hall (2005)
Paperback: 255 pages

Rule #1: The Simple Strategy for Successful Investing in Only 15 Minutes a Week by Phil Town
Publisher: Three Rivers Press (2007)
Paperback: 330 pages

Beating the Street: by Peter Lynch
Publisher: Simon & Schuster (1993)
Hardcover: 318 pages

What Works on Wall Street: The Classic Guide to the Best-Performing Investment Strategies of All Time by James P. O'Shaughnessy
Publisher: McGraw Hill (2012)
Hardcover: 681 pages

Getting Started in Options by Michael Thomsett
Publisher: John Wiley & Sons (2007)
Paperback: 383 pages

Options Made Easy: Your Guide to Profitable Trading by Guy Cohen
Publisher: FT Press (2005)
Hardcover: 335 pages

All About Market Indicators: The Easy Way to Get Started by Michael Sincere Publisher: McGraw Hill (2011)
Paperback: 217 pages

Buy High Sell Higher: Why Buy-AND-Hold Is Dead & Other Investing Lessons from CNBC's "The Liquidator" by Joe Terranova
Publisher: Business Plus (2012)
Hardcover: 261 pages

Buy and Hedge: The 5 Iron Rules for Investing Over the Long Term by Jay Pestrichelli & Wayne Ferbert
Publisher: FT Press (2012)
Hardcover: 289 pages

The Ultimate Dividend Playbook by Josh Peters
Publisher: John Wiley & Sons (2008)
Hardcover: 352 pages

Exit Strategies for Covered Calls by Alan Ellman
Publisher: Wheatmark (2009)
Paperback: 178 pages

Cashing in on Covered Calls by Alan Ellman
Publisher: SAMR Productions (2007)
Paperback: 392 pages

New Insights on Covered Call Writing by Richard Lehman & Lawrence McMillan
Publisher: Bloomberg Press (2003)
Hardcover: 240 pages

Stock Trader's Almanac by Jeffrey Hirsch & Yale Hirsch
Publisher: John Wiley & Sons
Hardcover: 192 pages

High Probability Trading by Marcel Link
Publisher: McGraw Hill (2003)
Hardcover: 393 pages

Unfair Advantage: The Power of Financial Education by
Robert Kiyosaki
Publisher: Plata Publishing (2011)
Paperback: 275 pages

The Millionaire Fastlane by MJ DeMarco
Publisher: Viperion (2011)
Paperback: 322 pages

32411940R00171

Made in the USA
San Bernardino, CA
13 April 2019